The Public Infrastructure
of Work and Play

THE URBAN AGENDA

Series Editor, Michael A. Pagano

A list of books in the series appears at the end of this book.

The Public Infrastructure of Work and Play

EDITED BY MICHAEL A. PAGANO

University of Illinois at Chicago

PUBLISHED FOR THE
COLLEGE OF URBAN PLANNING
AND PUBLIC AFFAIRS (CUPPA),
UNIVERSITY OF ILLINOIS AT CHICAGO,
BY THE UNIVERSITY OF ILLINOIS PRESS
Urbana, Chicago, and Springfield

The College of Urban Planning and Public Affairs of the University of Illinois at Chicago and the University of Illinois Press gratefully acknowledge that publication of this book was assisted by a grant from the John D. and Catherine T. MacArthur Foundation.

Library of Congress Control Number: 2018945717
ISBN 978-0-252-04215-7 (hardcover)
ISBN 978-0-252-08387-7 (paperback)
ISBN 978-0-252-05089-3 (e-book)

Contents

Preface and Acknowledgments

It was widely believed at the beginning of the Trump presidency that Congress would prepare a massive infrastructure bill. The president campaigned on a platform that promised $1 billion in new infrastructure spending that would engage the private sector in public-private partnerships as well as state and local governments. Infrastructure programs in the eyes of most were bipartisan in nature, the "crumbling infrastructure" dilemma challenged both red and blue states, and the public was broadly supportive. In anticipation of the nation's political conversation about the design of such a program, the UIC Urban Forum was convened in September 2017 around the broad issue of the state of our nation's urban and regional infrastructure.

Public infrastructure is the "built environment" that allows cities to thrive. By shaping and molding the cityscape and the growth patterns of the urban landscape, and by providing places for work, play, relaxation, cultural events, and community gatherings, cities are dependent on wise public infrastructure investment. From "hard infrastructure," such as public buildings, roads and bridges, dams and canals, to "soft infrastructure," such as parks and town squares, public art and rails-to-trails, a city's overall infrastructure has a significant influence on daily life and links its residents, neighborhoods, and businesses.

These features drive economic development and growth and serve to improve residents' quality of life. However, planning of projects where people work and play, and making well-designed connections between both, creates political challenges due to the intersection of public policy, markets, and aesthetics. Both hard and soft infrastructures have an impact that is felt for generations.

Given the important role that a city's infrastructure can have on its future viability, the 2017 UIC Urban Forum was designed to raise issues related to hard and soft infrastructures and how to unite them, the built environment's lasting effect on a city and its people, opportunities for economic development, and the future of city planning and design.

The 2017 UIC Urban Forum was cochaired by Cook County Board president Toni Preckwinkle and UIC chancellor Michael Amiridis. The event was held on September 14, 2017, and attracted four hundred students, community activists, private citizens, government and nonprofit leaders, and many others. The opening keynote address was presented by the renowned architect Carol Barney Ross and the closing keynote by the secretary of transportation for the state of Illinois, Randy Blankenhorn.

The first of the two panels was titled "Building a Just City: Shaping Communities' Quality of Life." Parks, public art, and architectural design are a critical piece of a city's aesthetics. These amenities can help inspire economic investment and make a positive impact on an urban community's physical and emotional condition. Creating future projects, both large and small, that ensure influential cultural developments are located and experienced across the City of Big Shoulders must be a priority. The panelists were as follows: Gia Biagi, principal, Studio Gang; Miguel Aguilar, artist; Juanita Irizarry, executive director, Friends of the Parks; and Scott Stewart, executive director, Millennium Park Foundation. The session was moderated by Alexandra Salomon, editor, *Curious City*, WBEZ.

The second panel was titled "Connecting People and Places: Designing Transportation Systems for Smart Cities." From roads to planes and bike lanes to trains, Chicago's status as a transportation hub is a foundational cornerstone of the region's economic engine. Government agencies, urban planners, and grassroots organizations must strategically connect and evolve transportation systems not only to maintain the city's standing but also to prepare for the future needs of its residential and business communities. Panelists were as follows: MarySue Barrett, president, Metropolitan Planning Council; Ron Burke, executive director, Active Transportation Alliance; Clayton Harris III, executive director, Illinois International Port District; and Leanne Redden, executive director, Regional Transportation Authority. The panel was moderated by Miles Bryan, reporter and producer, WBEZ.

The success of the conference is the product of numerous individuals who dedicated considerable time, energy, and ideas to the program. They include Jennifer Woodard, Norma Ramos, Brian Flood, Jantel Hines, and Karla Bailey of Jasculca Terman Strategic Communications. The support and event-planning skills of Jenny Sweeney are nonpareil and were critical to the conference's success. Casey Sebetto, a graduate student in the Department of Urban Planning and Policy, admirably undertook editorial assistance and manuscript supervision.

The 2017 UIC Urban Forum's external board of advisers included the following: Clarence Anthony, executive director, National League of Cities; MarySue Barrett, president, Metropolitan Planning Council; Henry Cisneros, former secretary of the Department of Housing and Urban Development, former mayor of San Antonio, and founder and chairman of CityView; Rahm Emanuel, mayor, Chicago; Lee Fisher, president and CEO, CEOs for Cities; Karen Freeman-Wilson, mayor, Gary; Bruce Katz, Centennial Scholar, Brookings Institution; Jeff Malehorn, president and CEO, World Business Chicago; Terry Mazany, president and CEO, Chicago Community Trust; Toni Preckwinkle, president, Cook County Board; Julia Stasch, president, John D. and Catherine T. MacArthur Foundation; Joseph Szabo, executive director, Chicago Metropolitan Agency for Planning; and Susana Vasquez, vice president for strategic initiatives and resource development, Illinois Facilities Fund.

The annual UIC Urban Forum offers thought-provoking, engaged, and insightful conferences on critical urban issues in a venue to which all of the world's citizens are invited.

Michael A. Pagano

Director of the UIC Urban Forum and Dean, College of Urban Planning and Public Affairs, University of Illinois at Chicago

February 2018

[blank page x]

PART ONE
OVERVIEW

[blank page 2]

The "Infrastructural Ideal"

Expansive, Contested, Eroding

PHILIP ASHTON

As the theme of the 2017 UIC Urban Forum suggests, we are living in an "infrastructural moment" in the United States. Public concern over a crumbling "hard" infrastructure fills newspapers, blog posts, and think-tank reports. Calls for widespread investment in new and enhanced urban infrastructure come from across the political landscape, drawing on the notion that "public capital" is essential to both economic development and growth as well as improvements in residents' quality of life. These outcries reference not just roads and bridges but also increasingly "soft" infrastructures of creativity—arts, cultural institutions, public space, and amenities—seen as central to economic growth and innovation in some corners. In certain cases, these calls reference cutting-edge infrastructural systems and technologies (such as driverless cars) that have yet to be invented.

At the same time, the legacies of earlier investments in public capital—both hard and soft—have become political flash points in new and unexpected ways. These conflicts do not always focus on the standard elements of politics—was decision making transparent, and was the project delivered on time and on budget?—but often hinge on symbolic and aesthetic elements, including the founding myths and imagined communities that underpin the "public" in the notion of public capital. The contemporary controversy over Confederate monuments serves as a direct reminder that investments in public capital ostensibly designed to tap a civic spirit can just as easily produce conflict and division.[1]

In this overview, I will lay out a set of themes that encompassed the more specific approaches taken by other authors participating in the forum. A

central theme that runs throughout this volume is the notion of the "infrastructural ideal" that animates current aspirations and debates over urban
infrastructure.[2] This ideal has several components, the most important being
that it draws together hard and soft infrastructures through a belief in the
positive social benefits of public capital. From the late nineteenth century
onward, this ideal proved to be an expansive one, encompassing new forms
of infrastructure as part of a progressive vision of the urban economy and
polity. Nevertheless, the ideal has a number of fault lines that have made
infrastructural investments controversial or politically contentious.

THE "INFRASTRUCTURAL IDEAL"

Presidential campaigns over the past thirty years have been replete with
calls for increased attention to urban infrastructure. As a recent example,
candidate Trump made investment in infrastructure a central plank of his
platform, calling for nearly $1 trillion in new investment to make the nation's
infrastructure "second to none." Trump's focus on infrastructure investment
was just the latest in a line of campaign pronouncements. As Democratic
nominee in 1994, Bill Clinton proposed $80 billion in federal spending on
roads and mass transit through a "Rebuild America Fund." Labeling this
spending "an investment" rather than simply deficit spending, candidate
Clinton argued that "the 1980s saw the concrete foundations of the United
States crumble" and called for significant federal spending on infrastructure to "help put Americans back to work and spur economic growth." In
2016 Democratic presidential nominee Hillary Clinton echoed this approach
with a proposed $275 billion package of infrastructure spending, stating, "In
America, we build great things together—from the transcontinental railroad
to the interstate highway system to the Hoover Dam."[3]

Even presidents whose pronouncements on infrastructure were more
subdued echoed concerns over investment. "Adequate and well-maintained
infrastructure is critical to economic growth," wrote George H. W. Bush in
1992 in an executive order incentivizing the privatization of "infrastructure
assets" (defined as "any asset financed in whole or in part by the Federal
Government and needed for the functioning of the economy"). For President
George W. Bush, the emphasis shifted post-9/11 to "critical infrastructure,"
"including emergency preparedness communications, and the physical assets that support such systems" that are both essential to national security
and most prone to disruption through terrorist attacks.[4]

These programmatic proposals all point to an increasingly pressing reality
for Americans: the material networks that facilitate economic activity and

mobility are in crisis, having in large measure been built in the seventy-year period between 1890 and 1960. One estimate, by the American Society of Civil Engineers, projects that the country will need "$3.6 trillion in public investment by 2020."[5] However, these campaign proposals are more than just calls to avoid a crisis of collapsing roads and bridges. They are simultaneously aspirational, referencing what Graham and Marvin have called a "modern infrastructural ideal" that connects infrastructure investment to growth, modernization, and economic progress—the "belief that, by promoting circulation, infrastructures bring about change, and through change they enact progress, and through progress we gain freedom."[6]

Even as there are a variety of physical forms and modes of provision that can be encompassed within this ideal, the distinctions between forms is less important for "infrastructural idealists" than is the shared role they play in economic and social life. O'Neill addresses this role by elaborating the economic arguments that separate out infrastructure as a good or service with special "publicness" characteristics. One set of characteristics focuses on infrastructure's universal availability and accessibility as a means of "[coordinating] and [sequencing] time with urban activities and household routines in concordance." Other characteristics include the inherent interconnection (bundling) among infrastructural systems such that "access to any infrastructure item guarantees access to others, and so that all infrastructure items can deliver publicly in complementary fashion." The urban street is, for O'Neill, an exemplar here. Even as the street is a jumble of different technical systems—roads, sidewalks, sewers, water mains, lighting, electrical and communications lines, and so on—those "basic infrastructure items can be bundled so that every household has coordinated use of the whole package. Moreover, it is generally impossible, and often illegal, for a householder not to have access to the complete, braided set."[7]

For economists, these forms of public capital sit apart from other forms of economic activity, as their provision is not coordinated by private markets. Nevertheless, the infrastructural ideal draws on a set of economic concepts to situate public capital as fundamental to economic growth. The most direct mechanisms here are *externalities*, wherein the production of an infrastructural good "has unintended impact on the utility or production function of another individual or firm,"[8] producing "[benefits] that [flow] to those other than to the parties involved directly in the transaction."[9] As Beverly Bunch notes in her contribution to this collection, the 1980s brought an increasing focus on the precise measurement—often through econometric modeling—of externalities and the multiplier effects of specific infrastructure transactions. For Gramlich, these studies brought the economic rate of return or "profit" of investments in public capital to the forefront of public debate.[10] This focus on the relationship between public capital and economic productivity parses increasingly fine lines between different forms of infrastructure transactions and their rate of return to specific users.[11] For instance, in the wake of the American Recovery and Reinvestment Act of 2009 (the Obama administration's "stimulus" package, which pumped $111 billion into infrastructural and science projects),[12] there has been a robust debate over whether the legislation erred in emphasizing "shovel ready" projects to promote short-term job creation over more visionary or long-term investments in high-speed rail, alternative energy, or fiber-optic networks.[13]

However, these conventional economic arguments—public goods and externalities—reference only two aspects of economic theory used to defend investments in public capital. To fully apprehend the nature of the infrastructural ideal, however, we need to assess those investments from within two alternative economic theories: those rooted in Marshallian evolutionary economics and those drawing on theories of the commons.

For the English economic historian Alfred Marshall, the externalities accompanying expanding infrastructural systems were more than simply transactional. "Every cheapening of the means of communication, every new facility for the free interchange of ideas between distant places," he stated in his seminal *Principles of Economics*, "alters the action of the forces which tend to localize industries." Whereas the spread of canals, roadways, rail, and other infrastructures of movement may have facilitated the purchase of goods from far-flung locations, it also "tends to bring skilled artisans to ply their crafts near to the consumers who will purchase their wares."[14] This dynamic of specialization—the concentration of specialized workers and producers in specific cities—was fundamental to the urbanization economies that lay at the center of Marshall's evolutionary theory of economic growth.

This is a different argument regarding the social wealth–enhancing effects of infrastructural investment than that found in narrowly transactional accounts debated by mainstream economists. As in William Cronon's history of Chicago, where the integration of rail systems in the second half of the nineteenth century produces a "second nature" capable of reorganizing economic relationships, the infrastructures that facilitate communication and mobility were essential to the creation of Marshall's fabled "thickly peopled industrial [districts]," wherein "mysteries of the trade become no mysteries, but are as it were in the air, and children learn many of them unconsciously."[15] Stated differently, the external economies of urban infrastructural investment must be seen as expansive, connecting the transactional to the systemic: "For each and every individual water and sewerage customer, for example, there is, concomitantly, a safe, hygienic city. From the power stations and electricity grids constructed to light and heat homes, there is also vast access to industrial power by manufacturers. From a road system that steers traffic onto efficient arterial roads there are (or there should be) quiet, safe suburban streets. And for (and, indeed, because of) every public transport user, there is cleaner air and there are fewer greenhouse gas emissions."[16]

A second alternative economic theory highlighting the social wealth–enhancing effects of infrastructural investment focuses on how hard physical infrastructures are deeply enmeshed in civic virtues. Amin has referred to this quality as the "liveliness" of infrastructure, arguing that infrastructure's "mundane socio-technicalities . . . are fundamental in shaping wellbeing, sociality, and organization."[17] Drawing on other threads of thinking from branches of law, economics, and anthropology, arguments about infrastructure's liveliness reference an *urban commons*[18]—one that both *creates* and *depends on* a shared public realm that is undifferentiated by property claims. For legal scholar Carol Rose, the efficiency of hard infrastructure, such as roadways and waterways, is dependent on a kind of "custom," whereby users abide by informal norms of co-occupation and use.[19] Imagine the complexities of merging lanes on an interstate highway to accommodate summertime construction, and one begins to see how efficient movement of people and goods (not to mention the possibility of maintenance and upkeep, which necessitate temporary disruptions) depends on a set of social norms and customs. Similar customs might include yielding to faster traffic, use of turn signals when passing, or avoiding use of high-beam headlights with oncoming traffic. Even as these conventions may seem like minor, even insignificant, gestures, they are nevertheless crucial to the efficient functioning of infrastructural systems. Further, because custom is essential to efficiency, it is central to the externalities celebrated by the infrastructural ideal.

To take another example, consider Internet and communications technology. Even as the Internet is popularly characterized as a deterritorialized "space of flows," it relies on extensive fixed investments in private and public capital to create the "virtual" spaces where users interact.[20] This form of infrastructure was a significant focus of urban investment under Clinton-era "digital commons" programs, emphasizing the digital divide and community technology centers.[21] Yet the viability of the Internet—as a virtual community or as a commercial endeavor—depends on the attention of users, attention that is increasingly scarce (a function of the overwhelming proliferation of

Web-based opportunities) or that is made fragile by destructive behaviors such as trolling.[22]

Attention and custom exceed formal law; they cannot be easily codified, they must be learned through repeated use, and policing would likely be a costly and difficult endeavor. Indeed, their very publicness qualifies the infrastructural spaces where they are operative as a "commons" that can function efficiently only by virtue of a set of civic habits shared by users. Like all forms of common property, they are subject to erosion as individual users seek advantage by flaunting custom. (Those who have driven Michigan interstates in midsummer, where drivers are packed into the passing lane, all seeking a faster arrival at their vacation destination, have experienced what this is like.) As debates over the digital commons and net neutrality (the notion that pricing mechanisms cannot be used to make Internet access scarce based on ability to pay) further reinforce, there are active questions over how regulation can best sustain the equal access necessary for "lively" infrastructure. For her part, Rose sees a selective emergence of legal protections of the shared public realm of infrastructure through "strong doctrines" of public protection; however, these doctrines seem narrow and applicable only to infrastructures such as roads and waterways.[23]

AN EXPANSIVE IDEAL: HARD AND SOFT INFRASTRUCTURE

As the chapters in this volume all note, the question of what counts as infrastructure looms large in contemporary arguments regarding an infrastructural crisis. Sanjeev Vidyarthi, for instance, notes in this volume the distinction between utilities, facilities, and public works, each working at different scales or with a different role in economic life. Indeed, as there has been an increasing specialization of urban infrastructure following shifts in the underlying nature of economic activity and competition, so too have disciplines of economics and public policy developed greater theoretical precision to assess and describe the various externalities that accompany new forms of hard infrastructure.

Notwithstanding this ever more narrow and specialized approach to economic externalities and multipliers, the infrastructural ideal has proved to be an expansive one. As Charlie Hoch notes in his chapter in this volume, throughout the heyday of the industrial city, the infrastructural ideal grew to encompass more than just hard infrastructural systems essential to economic growth. In this section, I want to anticipate Hoch's arguments regarding the "infrastructure of play" to focus on one thread of that expansion, whereby new forms of soft public capital have come to be accommodated under the heading of infrastructure. One aspect of this expansion involved the increasingly overt connection between investment in certain forms of public capital and imagined notions (and norms) of democratic community that are produced as "externalities" by those investments.

For American pragmatists such as John Dewey, the norms of growth and prosperity that underpinned economic expansion in the late nineteenth and early twentieth centuries were fundamentally wrapped up in a set of liberal democratic impulses that necessitated their own forms of infrastructure. Economic growth and social progress were seen to be fundamentally tied to one another, both through the norms of progress but also through the infrastructural instinct rooted in Progressive Era bureaucracies. One form of public capital that was central to the link between growth and social progress was the public school. Dewey focused on public schools as essential to training youth into the moral habits of citizenry, making the universal accessibility of the physical plant of primary and secondary schools a key marker of progress to a better society. Even as large schools came to be associated with social control and the reproduction of an ordered working class,[24] there remained an aspiration that the public school could be a physical space capable of "another task: that of making the community as a whole capable of controlling its destinies."[25] For his part, Dewey spoke passionately about overcoming "the difference between the school as an isolated thing related to the state alone, and the school as a thoroughly socialized affair in contact at all points with the flow of community."[26] In this role of enhancing community self-determination, the public school was joined by "accessory" institutions, including "the public library and reading room, public workshops, studios, and laboratories, and public dance-halls and little theaters," whose small scale and orientation toward a neighborhood might make them "physical facilities for a good social life" and key to the "new biotechnic regime based on the deliberate culture of life."[27]

> I suppose, whenever we are framing our ideals of the school as a social center, what we think of particularly is the better class of social settlements. What we want is to see the school, every public school, doing something of the same sort of work that is now done by a settlement or two scattered at wide distances through the city. We all know that the function of such an institution as Hull House has been primarily not that of conveying intellectual instruction, but of being a social clearinghouse. It is not merely a place where ideas and beliefs may be exchanged in the arena of formal discussion, for argument alone breeds misunderstanding and fixes prejudice; but it is much

more a place where ideas are incarnated in human form and clothed with the winning grace of personal life. Classes for study may be numerous, but they are regarded as modes of bringing people together, of doing away with the barriers of caste or class or race or type of experience that keep people from real communion with each other.[28]

The public school was not the only form of soft infrastructure that demonstrated democratic externalities in this way. Investments in public space have similarly been important to contemporary theorizing about urban democracy.[29] As Charlie Hoch notes in his chapter "Infrastructure of Urban Play," parks and playgrounds were seen as critical to the health and welfare of the nation by late-nineteenth- and early-twentieth-century urban reformers. For organizations such as the American Park and Outdoor Art Association (formed in 1893) or the American League for Civic Improvement (founded in 1902), not only were green spaces remedies to the pollution and congestion of the industrial city, but they also formed the basis for democratic encounter between social classes or between native and immigrant.[30] Notwithstanding the patronizing subtext of much of these reform organizations—which saw advocacy of parks and green space grounded in the need for moral uplift on the part of the poor—outdoor spaces became a key part of the public sphere or the public patrimony. Nor were these arguments limited to a set of Progressive Era reformers. Sennett echoes a significant strand of contemporary urban theory when he argues that public space remains a "site that offers relief from the burdens of subjective life" that facilitates "mutual engagement, and so mutual obligation and loyalty."[31]

Fused to a growing rational bureaucracy within large Progressive Era cities, this expansive infrastructural ideal gave rise to a particular form of urban life. Walking the streets of New York City, to take a prominent example, one gets a sense of how concerted investment in public capital transformed the experiences of residents who only decades earlier might have been crowded into the city's tenements. Alongside the system of thoroughfares, bridges, and tunnels—the hard infrastructure so prized by city builder Robert Moses[32]—we find the neighborhood handball and basketball courts and the network of pocket parks and swimming pools, the solidity of elementary and secondary schools or the city's public library system, and the edifices of the City University of New York (once free and considered the "blue-collar Harvard"). These forms of public capital and the institutions that support them may not have radically transformed the economic circumstances of tenement residents, but they nonetheless remain a distinguishing and important physical and social element of the city.

Moreover, the expansion of infrastructural ideal was based on more than neighborhood institutions or open spaces alone. Arts and cultural institutions rode on the coattails of expanding physical networks of roads, rails, and communications, with advocates arguing that these forms of soft infrastructure similarly "delivered other benefits, such as binding the social and cultural activity of a city."[33] Certain urban reformers may have been less interested in museums, galleries, symphonies, or opera houses, as they seemed removed from the ideals of rationalizing the industrial city or assimilating the exploding migrant population into a nascent urban democracy. Nevertheless, by the heyday of the industrial city—from 1880 through the Great Depression—arts and cultural institutions in U.S. cities were proliferating through substantial patronage by urban elites.[34] This patronage had a hard dimension, in the form of monumental museum buildings, opera houses, or symphony halls, often paid for through public subscription. The benefits of these physical investments were perhaps more nebulous than other hard infrastructure or public institutions such as schools, but by positioning the city as a "cosmopolitan place filled with cultural offerings," commercial elites could engage in the symbolic competition for position with a shifting hierarchy of places.[35] That is, economic growth was seen as fundamentally tied to a set of nonproductive investments in public patrimony. Further, as long as these institutions were funded by private philanthropy, and as long as symbolic competition was seen as central to competitive advantage, they benefited from broad-based support from urban elites.

The example of the Art Institute of Chicago is illustrative. Originally created in the 1860s as an artist-run residential organization, by the late 1870s it had run into financial and management problems. When a group of commercial and financial leaders were brought in to serve on a board of trustees, they forced "a decisive shift from a school run by artists to a multifaceted institution superintended by the city's mercantile elite." They emphasized developing a collection of art that "mirrored the ambitions and tastes of the institute's leaders . . . reflecting beliefs that a civic museum should feature masterpieces, a category then meaning original artworks from Europe."[36] A new building, erected on a prominent lakefront site in 1893 and financed by real estate deals and public subscriptions,[37] announced the patrician aims of the institute's patrons with a Beaux-Arts design that mimicked the great museums of London (the Victoria and Albert) and Paris (the Louvre).[38] The new institution was seen as so important to the city's status that Aaron Montgomery Ward dropped his staunch opposition to development in Grant Park in order to have the museum see the light of day.[39]

A CONTESTED IDEAL: GROWTH MACHINES
AND DIVISIVE SYMBOLISM

Even as the ideals of investment in public capital expanded to encompass schools, public space, and arts and cultural institutions, that expansion was divisive and controversial. The very production of large-scale urban infrastructure is often destructive of the urban social fabric it seeks to enhance; to take a direct example in Chicago, critical roadways such as the Dan Ryan and Kennedy Expressways and key public investments such as the University of Illinois's Chicago Circle campus (now UIC) were possible only through a massive campaign of property expropriation and neighborhood demolition. That these urban renewal campaigns were orchestrated by self-interested urban growth machines seeking to reward powerful political constituencies added only insult to injury. The enrollment of museums, cultural institutions, and anchor institutions, such as universities, as advocates for (or beneficiaries of) urban renewal further delegitimized the link between investments in public capital and the public good.

The notion that infrastructural investments would produce social conflicts, even as they seek to unite urban populations, was not limited to the urban renewal period. In the context of heightened intermunicipal competition since the 1970s, "creative city" discourses have reoriented urban development policy toward forms of public capital with "the capacity to attract, retain and even pamper a mobile and finicky class of 'creatives,' whose aggregate efforts have become the primary drivers of economic development" in the postindustrial era. In the eyes of creative-city advocates, the critical infrastructures for urban economic growth are no longer bundled and universal, emphasizing communication, business location, or the least cost for movement of goods and services, but rather those that enhance the "creative ecosystem" and "people climate" attractive to a new dynamic class of creative workers and entrepreneurs. What kinds of infrastructure align with wooing and retaining the creative class? According to Peck, creatives seek "the kind of amenities that allow them precariously to maintain a work-life balance, together with experiential intensity, in the context of those demanding work schedules."[40] As these often encompass the soft infrastructure of arts and culture, with lower needs for public investment compared to sports stadia or convention centers, they have proved popular with cash-strapped municipalities looking to harness "infrastructures of play" for economic development.[41]

However, in their concrete forms, these amenities share several controversial features. They tend to be geographically limited; rather than being spread equitably throughout the city, they tend to emphasize areas where creatives cluster, such as affluent neighborhoods or emerging entertainment districts. They also often emphasize the leisure or consumption preferences of this small segment of the population: "Play and consumption really matter here because creatives confront the unique challenge of fitting these in around their demanding work schedules, squeezing in a quick bike ride or latte at the art gallery before starting the second shift." Finally, as creatives are drawn to the "symbols of urban authenticity," which "include 'authentic' historical buildings, converted lofts, walkable streets, plenty of coffeeshops, art and live music spaces, [and] 'organic and indigenous street culture,'" investments in public capital in support of the creative city often spur or reinforce gentrification and the displacement of low-income residents and businesses.[42] To the degree that municipalities are increasingly pursuing creative-city strategies for economic development, they have embraced investments in public capital with a significant capacity for controversy.

The recent storm over Chicago's "606 Trail"—a rail-to-trail project on the city's northwest side—offers an example. The 2.7-mile trail was originally conceived as a linear park that could remedy open-space disparities in the low-income Latino neighborhoods of Logan Square and Humboldt Park. Its design elements carried a substantial "cool" factor, capitalizing on the site's status as a former industrial rail spur and promising new connections for cyclists. However, by linking gentrified Bucktown and Wicker Park to the east with a set of low-income neighborhoods to the west, the trail has reframed perceptions of those neighborhoods' desirability.[43] The result has been a development rush, with a slew of new high-end condo and rental projects seeking to capitalize on the allure of proximity to the trail.[44] Whereas neighborhood groups initially focused on advocacy for the trail, they have now turned to organizing protests against land grabs by developers and the displacement of low-income renters.[45] The controversy has shaped new awareness on the part of housing and community advocates in other parts of the city of the socially divisive aspects of "cool" industrial reclamation projects.[46]

Another set of recent controversies—this time over public monuments to the Confederacy—has further served to remind us of another divisive aspect of public capital, namely, that it is often cloaked in a symbolism capable of fracturing the very integrative aspirations of the infrastructural ideal. Here, the focus shifts from the validation of public capital's economic role to its affective and aesthetic qualities and "how public sentiments of progress, modernity and wellbeing become attached to iconic buildings, highways, or new housing and shopping complexes, regardless of their functionality and material impact." In examples such as the Art Institute of Chicago or other monumental edifices, the "emblematic material" references "an imagined commons of shared affects and assets supposed to iron out the divisions and differences of the everyday city."[47] Nevertheless, this symbolic power is always socially selective. In the case of Confederate monuments, municipal and state governments from the late nineteenth through the mid-twentieth centuries enhanced their standing through the mobilization of symbols referencing founding stories of the Confederacy and its imagined community of white southerners.[48] In the wake of a wave of political protest around police treatment of minorities or local deference to white supremacists, those symbols now stand as physical monuments to a divided polity.

AN ERODING IDEAL?

Even as the infrastructural ideal has been promoted through election campaign rhetoric dating back at least to the early 1990s, the underlying vision of infrastructure referenced by that rhetoric—integrated, innovative, universally accessible, essential to economic livelihood, and linked to the democratic public sphere—has been much harder to find at the programmatic level. Why has the infrastructural ideal receded from the policy landscape even as it retains such a significant rhetorical hold? There are at least two arguments we can examine to better understand the gap between the belief in the efficacy of infrastructure and the reality of shrinking investment: the turn to austerity urbanism and the "assetization" of public capital through successive waves of privatization.

Austerity Urbanism

Fiscal circumstances have certainly worked to exacerbate the sense that integrated infrastructure is in a crisis. The 1975 New York City fiscal crisis was a signal moment in this regard, helping to usher in a new set of controls on spending and borrowing that marked a decisive shift away from the city's postwar commitment to public capital.[49] The turn to austerity urbanism not only diminished new investments and ongoing upkeep of hard infrastructure but also increasingly targeted soft infrastructure as unsustainable in the face of increasing pressures on the public fisc.[50]

Moreover, austerity urbanism has specifically targeted one pillar of the integrated infrastructural ideal: its reliance on a public-sector monopoly. For

Graham and Marvin, the broad-based public qualities to urban infrastructure were sustained by their institutional location, situated as they were within the emerging modern professions of urban planning and public administration.[51] Just as important, the infrastructural ideal was sustained by the consolidation of the legal authority of the municipal corporation,[52] which helped produce "public infrastructure monopolies" as part of Progressive Era apparatus of the local state. For O'Neill, these monopolies were central to the emergence of a Keynesian "infrastructure instinct" in the postwar period—a set of infrastructural capacities that flowed from "public acceptance of infrastructure funding and rollout as essential to the conduct of modern society." Whether housed in public works agencies or in quasi–public monopoly utilities, the design, delivery, and maintenance of infrastructure systems became central capacities for a bureaucracy whose role and status grew as "capital works funding [became] a fixed category in the pages of government budgets." With unionization of frontline workers, this capacity became entrenched in collective bargaining arrangements as part of "an infrastructure profession—with its skills, documents, books and working implements," capable of "[ensuring] a reliable and continuous corporate memory of how to create and enact infrastructure projects in an orderly, sequenced and continuous fashion."[53] As public monopolies and public-sector unionization have come under attack as inefficient and fiscally unsustainable, this memory and its attendant capacity have been eroded.

Turning Infrastructure into a Financial Asset

The attack on public agencies and public workers did not result in a smaller bureaucracy dedicated to infrastructure provision. Rather, O'Neill notes "a persistent and significant re-engagement with infrastructure inside the state apparatus over at least the last two decades." What has shifted is the form of that bureaucracy and the way that it approaches investment in public capital. In the United States, this shift began in the Reagan administration, which created a Commission on Privatization in 1987 to examine ways to "return government programs and assets to the people."[54] In the early 1990s under President Bush, these initiatives were picked up in more specific proposals and incentives to privatize infrastructure assets. The economic arguments mobilized in favor of privatization of infrastructure were threefold: private owners and operators have inherent efficiencies that public-sector operators lack, a belief in the pricing mechanism as a more efficient means of allocating infrastructure than general taxation,[55] and a claim that public financing of infrastructure crowded out private investment, acting as "a barrier to the achievement of economic efficiencies through additional private market financing or competitive practices, or both."[56]

Early state initiatives to privatize new road construction (for instance, in Virginia) retained a public utilities model, with private operators facing regulation by a state commission. However, states and localities quickly found that such an approach had limits and that private investment was most likely to flow when infrastructure was structured as an unrestricted private commodity. Even as shifts toward this model were often grounded in economic arguments regarding the efficiency of private-sector operation, or even more fundamentally in the superiority of the pricing mechanism (such as the toll) as a means of allocating public goods, they had broader effects not anticipated by their boosters. Most notably, they involved an underlying shift in the very notion of infrastructure. "This is a shift from a device capable of generating (and then the financing, construction and provision) a public-capital good, based on a concept infused with universality; and designed to integrate cities and regions, add cohesion to social and economic communities, provide free positive externalities, counteract or minimise the negative externalities of private pursuits of the city—like driving a private motor car—and, when required, deliver Keynesian economic stimulus, via the construction sector, to lagging regions."[57]

Under successive waves of privatization, the notion of infrastructure that emerges is quite different: redefined as an "asset,"[58] each infrastructural item or subsystem becomes defined by its discrete earnings potential and by its risk-return profile relative to other large-scale, long-term private investment opportunities. Further, with the increasing role of investment banks in purchasing and financing infrastructure concessions in the 2000s, this earnings potential itself becomes a financial commodity, "capable of being bundled into repeated earnings-generating financial products."[59]

This assetization of urban infrastructure has implications on two fronts. First, it is highly selective, prioritizing those sectors or areas of the city that match investors' expectations regarding risk and return. It is also selective in the social sense. Private concessions often work by enhancing infrastructure's scarcity, employing steep increases in user fees to ensure appropriate revenue growth for investors.[60] In this way, it benefits those who have the financial means to pay for infrastructure, and it excludes those who cannot. Second, assetization actively works against the aspiration to bundled universal infrastructure. It creates barriers between infrastructural subsystems that impede integrated planning. Here, we can take yet another example from Chicago, that being the city's 2008 seventy-five-year lease of its street parking meters to a consortium led by the investment bank Morgan Stanley.[61] In handing over management of street parking to private operators, the city committed to ensuring that it did not affect the concessionaire's earnings stream through adverse events, such as street closures. Only a few years into the concession, this has exposed conflicts with key urban management functions—ranging from regular road maintenance to street festivals—that did not exist under earlier modes of service delivery. Further, monetizing the parking system as an infrastructure asset has created new barriers for integrated transportation planning; for instance, to the extent that bike lanes and bus rapid-transit initiatives would reduce the stock of parking spaces on certain arterials, they would require new financial commitments from the city to compensate private concessionaires—commitments that are increasingly difficult to justify under austerity urbanism.[62]

These fault lines suggest a particular bind for infrastructural politics for the twenty-first century. On the one hand, the infrastructural ideal seems as powerful as ever. The vagaries of global competition have made calls for investment in cutting-edge communication, energy, and logistics networks seem routine, with those calls drawing on notions of infrastructure's multiplier effects that directly channel Alfred Marshall. The ideal is also just as expansive as it was at the beginning of the last century. Creative-city advocates further channel Marshall in postulating that the key industrial districts of the twenty-first century, wherein "mysteries of the trade become no mysteries, but are as it were in the air, and children learn many of them unconsciously," are enclaves peopled with creatives drawn to the city for its lifestyle and amenities. For cities enthralled with the creative-city message, there is a direct line between planning for (and investing in) the soft infrastructure of arts and culture, or in neighborhood amenities that leverage urban authenticity, and being a contender for Amazon's second headquarters (HQ2).[63]

On the other hand, action toward infrastructural investment seems increasingly fragmented. Whether it is the locational conflicts over siting solar energy fields or wind farms, the fiscal politics that have accompanied rising bills for upkeep of "legacy" infrastructure,[64] the socially divisive effects of the creative-city agenda, or seemingly irreconcilable stances on the symbolism of major monuments, the notions of shared progress that sustained the infrastructural ideal in the twentieth century appear to have evaporated. And it is not just that it is harder to reach agreement on how infrastructural systems should work and for whom. Four decades of deficit politics have eroded the very idea of public capital that underlies integrated infrastructure and with it the public institutions and instincts that sustained that investment. Economists have entrenched the notion that public goods are prone to overproduction and that the price mechanism (charging user fees) is the best antidote to that problem. This has served to shift evaluation toward their robustness as earnings packages, in the process "unbundling" different infrastructural systems—and the commons that sustain them—from one another. Further, as increasing use of tolls and user fees splits users according to their ability to pay, public support has become fragmented between user groups based on their pecuniary attachments to specific kinds of infrastructure. The result is that "the bundled, coordinated city is therefore becoming the splintered city."[65]

Notes

1. "Confederate Monuments Are Coming Down across the United States," *New York Times*, August 16, 2017, https://www.nytimes.com/interactive/2017/08/16/us/confederate-monuments-removed.html?

2. Stephen Graham and Simon Marvin, *Splintering Urbanism: Networked Infrastructures, Technological Mobilities and the Urban Condition* (London: Routledge: 2001), 43.

3. Melanie Zanona, "Five Things to Know about Trump's Infrastructure Plan," *Hill*, November 20, 2016, http://thehill.com/policy/transportation/306847-five-things-to-know-about-trumps-infrastructure-plan; Stephen Chapman, "The False Promise of Clinton's Public Works 'Investment,'" *Chicago Tribune*, January 10, 1993, http://articles.chicagotribune.com/1993-01-10/news/9303160792_1_infrastructure-investment-mass-transit-spending; Hillary Clinton, "Fixing America's Infrastructure," 2016, https://www.hillaryclinton.com/issues/fixing-americas-infrastructure/.

4. George H. W. Bush, "Executive Order 12803—Infrastructure Privatization," April 30, 1992, http://www.presidency.ucsb.edu/ws/?pid=23625; George H. W. Bush, "Executive Order 13231—Critical Infrastructure Protection in the Information Age," October 16, 2001, http://www.presidency.ucsb.edu/ws/?pid=61512.

5. John Cassidy, "An Infrastructure Proposal That Goes beyond Clinton and Trump," August 17, 2016, http://www.newyorker.com/news/john-cassidy/an-infrastructure-proposal-that-goes-beyond-clinton-and-trump.

6. Graham and Marvin, *Splintering Urbanism*, 43; Brian Larkin, "The Politics of Poetics of Infrastructure," *Annual Review of Anthropology* 42 (2013): 332.

7. Phillip O'Neill, "Infrastructure Financing and Operation in the Contemporary City," *Geographical Research* 48, no. 1 (2010): 7.

8. Johan Fourie, "Economic Infrastructure: A Review of Definitions, Theory and Empirics," *South African Journal of Economics* 74, no. 3 (2006): 534.

9. O'Neill, "Infrastructure Financing and Operation," 8.

10. Edward M. Gramlich, "Infrastructure Investment: A Review Essay," *Journal of Economic Literature* 32, no. 3 (1994): 1176–96.

11. John G. Fernald, "Roads to Prosperity? Assessing the Link between Public Capital and Productivity," *American Economic Review* 89, no. 3 (1999): 619–38; Gramlich, "Infrastructure Investment."

12. Kevin Kliesen and Douglas Smith, "Digging into the Infrastructure Debate," *Regional Economist* (July 2009): 4–9.

13. Claudia Copeland, Linda Levine, and William J. Mallett, *The Role of Public Works Infrastructure in Economic Recovery* (Washington, DC: Congressional Research Service, 2011).

14. Alfred Marshall, *Principles of Economics: An Introductory Volume* (London: Royal Economic Society, 1890), 157.

15. William Cronon, *Nature's Metropolis: Chicago and the Great West* (New York: W. W. Norton, 1991); Marshall, *Principles of Economics*, 156.

16. O'Neill, "Infrastructure Financing and Operation," 8.

17. Ash Amin, "Lively Infrastructure," *Theory, Culture, and Society* 31, nos. 7–8 (2014): 138.

18. Christian Borch and Martin Kornberger, eds., *Urban Commons: Rethinking the City* (London: Routledge, 2016).

19. Carol Rose, *Property and Persuasion: Essays on the History, Theory, and Rhetoric of Ownership* (Boulder, CO: Westview Press, 1994).

20. Manuel Castells, *The Rise of the Network Society: The Information Age: Economy, Society, and Culture*, vol. 1 (London: Wiley-Blackwell, 1996).

21. Karen Mossberger, Caroline J. Tolbert, and Ramona S. McNeal, *Digital Citizenship: The Internet, Society, and Participation* (Cambridge, MA: MIT Press, 2007).

22. Tiziana Terranova, "Attention, Economy and the Brain," *Culture Machine* 13 (2012): 1–19.

23. Rose, *Property and Persuasion*.

24. John Dewey, "The School as Social Center," *Elementary School Teacher* 3, no. 2 (1902): 73–86.

25. Lewis Mumford, *The Culture of Cities* (New York: Harcourt, Brace, and Jovanovich, 1938), 476.

26. Dewey, "School as Social Center," 75.

27. Mumford, *The Culture of Cities*, 477, 9.

28. Dewey, "School as Social Center," 84.

29. Ash Amin and Nigel Thrift, *Cities: Reimagining the Urban* (London: Polity Press 2002).

30. Ibid., 133; M. Christine Boyer, *Dreaming the Rational City: The Myth of American City Planning* (Cambridge, MA: MIT Press, 1986).

31. Richard Sennett, "The Spaces of Democracy," in *Spaces of Culture: City—Nation—World*, ed. M. Featherstone and S. Lash (Sage: London, 1999), 23–24.

32. Robert Caro, *The Power Broker: Robert Moses and the Fall of New York* (New York: Alfred A. Knopf, 1972).

33. O'Neill, "Infrastructure Financing and Operation," 7.

34. William Sites, *Remaking New York* (Minneapolis: University of Minnesota Press, 2003).

35. Diane Dillon, "Art Institute of Chicago: The Electronic Encyclopedia of Chicago," 2005, http://www.encyclopedia.chicagohistory.org/pages/79.html.

36. Ibid.

37. Alice Sinkevitch, *AIA Guide to Chicago*, 2nd ed. (New York: Harcourt Books, 2004).

38. Dillon, "Art Institute of Chicago."

39. Sinkevitch, *AIA Guide to Chicago*, 14.

40. Jamie Peck, "Struggling with the Creative Class," *International Journal of Urban and Regional Research* 29, no. 4 (2005): 740, 743, 745.

41. Dennis Judd, ed., *The Infrastructure of Play: Building the Tourist City* (Armonk, NY: M. E. Sharpe, 2001).

42. Peck, "Struggling with the Creative Class," 745.

43. Lauren Nolan, "The 606, Gentrification, and the Future of Chicago's Northwest Side," Voorhees Center for Neighborhood and Community Improvement, 2015, https://voorheescenter.wordpress.com/2015/07/23/the-606-gentrification-and-the-future-of-chicagos-northwest-side/.

44. Geoff Smith et al., *Measuring the Impact of the 606: Understanding How a Large Public Investment Impacted the Surrounding Community* (Chicago: Institute for Housing Studies at DePaul University, 2016).

45. Genevieve Bookwalter, "Humboldt Park Protesters Fear Higher Housing Prices, Decry Loss of 1890s Home," *Chicago Tribune*, January 30, 2016, http://www.chicagotribune.com/news/local/breaking/ct-humboldt-park-bloomingdale-trail-protest-20160130-story.html.2016.

46. John Greenfield, "Little Village Residents Hope Paseo Won't Be a Path to Gentrification," *Chicago Reader*, March 23, 2016, https://www.chicagoreader.com/chicago/little-village-pilsen-paseo-displacement-fears/Content?oid=21527919.

47. Amin, "Lively Infrastructure," 138–39.

48. "Confederate Monuments Are Coming Down."

49. Sites, *Remaking New York*.

50. Jamie Peck and Heather Whiteside, "Financializing Detroit," *Economic Geography* 92, no. 3 (2016): 235–68.

51. Graham and Marvin, *Splintering Urbanism*, 43; cf. Boyer, *Dreaming the Rational City*.

52. Cf. Gerald E. Frug, "The City as a Legal Concept," *Harvard Law Review* 93, no. 6 (1980): 1057–1154.

53. O'Neill, "Infrastructure Financing and Operation," 5.

54. Ibid., 6; Joel Brinkley, "Reagan Appoints Privatization Unit," *New York Times*, September 4, 1987.

55. "User fees are generally more efficient than general taxes as a means to support infrastructure assets." Bush, "Executive Order 12803."

56. Ibid.

57. O'Neill, "Infrastructure Financing and Operation," 7.

58. Bush, "Executive Order 12803."

59. Phillip O'Neill, "Infrastructure Investment and the Management of Risk," in *Managing Financial Risks: From Global to Local*, ed. Gordon L. Clark, Adam D. Dixon, and Ashby H. B. Monk (Oxford: Oxford University Press, 2009), 175.

60. Philip Ashton, Marc Doussard, and Rachel Weber, "The Financial Engineering of Infrastructure Privatization: What Are Public Assets Worth to Private Investors?," *Journal of the American Planning Association* 78, no. 3 (2012): 300–312.

61. Philip Ashton, Marc Doussard, and Rachel Weber, "Reconstituting the State: City Powers and Exposures in Chicago's Infrastructure Leases," *Urban Studies* 53, no. 7 (2016): 1384–1400.

62. Stephanie Farmer, "Cities as Risk Managers: The Impact of Chicago's Parking Meter P3 on Municipal Governance and Transportation Planning," *Environment and Planning A* 46, no. 9 (2014): 2160–74.

63. Marshall, *Principles of Economics*, 156; Greg Hinz, "Here Are the Sites Chicago Is Pitching to Amazon," *Crain's Chicago Business*, October 20, 2017, http://www.chicago business.com/article/20171020/BLOGS02/171029972/here-are-the-sites-chicago-is -pitching-to-amazon.

64. Philip Ashton, "Legacy Costs in Infrastructure: Is the Cure Worse than the Disease?," in *Metropolitan Resilience in a Time of Economic Turmoil*, ed. Michael A. Pagano (Urbana: University of Illinois Press, 2014).

65. O'Neill, "Infrastructure Financing and Operation," 10.

[blank page 22]

PART TWO
WHITE PAPERS

[blank page 24]

Infrastructure of Urban Play

CHARLES HOCH

Each person learns to play within specific times and places. Think of the variety of places you used as a child hiding, chasing, exploring, swimming, jumping, climbing, throwing, catching, and on and on. In your early years, careful parents would warn you to avoid playing in the street or the stream. Alleyways proved more accessible. Climbing utility poles was unacceptable. The pickup games among neighborhood peers introduced complex environmental negotiations, marking out fields, arenas, courts, or other spaces for legitimate action on an empty field or lightly traveled street. Scripting the complex interactions among dolls, trucks, soldiers, guns, and costumed actors turned yards, sandboxes, basements, and places of every sort into playgrounds. Making processions and parades for resistant pets and toddlers, making music and dancing in fantasy studios—the imaginative repertoire of childhood play adapts to the spaces that adults create mostly for other purposes, some explicitly laid out as official rules and others embedded as traditional conventions.

We understand play in the United States in vivid contrast with work. The various meanings for play anticipate the free and spontaneous movement of the body for exercise, sport, pleasure, entertainment, and delight. Play describes the conduct of these sorts of actions within specific contexts and settings. These include gymnasiums, auditoriums, theaters, pools, halls, studios, and fields. Places for play in modern postindustrial societies rely on, and often take for granted, institutional and physical infrastructure.

In the United States, responsibility for the infrastructure of play includes public and private institutions. These institutions share authority for the construction, creation, and management of places for play. The plans and policies these institutions adopt and implement shape the contours that guide what and how people play. This chapter classifies how the most salient institutions exercise their responsibility and how this influences the social and spatial organization of play for people. I offer a framework that analyzes the type of play in relation to sponsorship. A quick sketch of the demand for different types of play introduces an overview of some problems and opportunities in the current spatial organization of the infrastructure for play. I offer examples from Chicago to illustrate. The conclusion describes innovations that may improve future infrastructure policy and investment.

REFORMERS LAY THE BASIC INFRASTRUCTURE FOR MODERN PLAY

The United States is obsessed with work as the measure of individual achievement and social value. Leisure distracts from the demands of labor and what jobs accomplish. It must be earned and then put to good use by purchasing entertainment that provides stress-relieving fun. The concept of play serving as its own reward, an action contributing to a more complete self and a better world, must instead be a hobby or a self-improvement project. The various meanings for play anticipate the free and spontaneous movement of the body for exercise, sport, pleasure, entertainment, and delight. Play describes the conduct of these sorts of actions within different contexts and settings. These include gymnasiums, auditoriums, theaters, pools, halls, studios, and fields. These places for play in modern societies rely on an often taken for granted institutional and physical infrastructure that emerged to cope with the excesses of industrial urbanization.

Nature and the Built Urban Environment

The Industrial Revolution fused the powers of the engineering sciences with the limitless ambition of capitalist accumulation. Just as Darwin's conception of evolution undermined belief in a transcendent human nature, the architecture of human purpose claimed the bounty of nature as a resource for ever-expanding economic and population growth. The infrastructure for agriculture, mining, manufacturing, transport, and consumption overwhelmed the compact spatial form of prior human settlements. Urbanization expanded at an unprecedented rate, grafted loosely onto the physical fabric of established cities or morphing tiny hamlets into sprawling settlements within a single human generation.

As economic markets for capital, labor, goods, services, and land proliferated and spread across the world, so too did the dramatic increases in wealth and the hierarchical segmentation and segregation of human populations into social classes, racial clusters, ethnic enclaves, and cultural niches. The modern urban settlements that encompassed and reinforced these changes did not behave with the predictability of the technical processes and institutional conventions that built them. Social conflicts and environmental problems emerged whose causes were unclear and solutions unknown. Reform efforts focused on these problems, combining knowledge from the sciences, humanities, and arts to comprehend the causes and solutions trying out contested conceptions of a public good.

Resistance and Assistance

The prominence of industrial agriculture and manufacturing transformed the lives of workers. Disciplined by the organized sequence of repeated tasks squeezed into a twelve-hour day, people did not learn a craft but performed a job. The manufacturing process generated exponential increases in the production of goods at the expense of the autonomy and competence of the individual worker. People embraced factory labor because they had few other alternatives. Most suffered from the physical and social exhaustion of the relentless pace of production. Many resisted fueling the emergence of labor unions whose members collaborated to protest the speed and danger of production and hold the threat of going on strike. The relentless imposition of labor discipline and the squalid density of slum dwellings left few places for play. Adults squeezed into what private open spaces they could find, men frequenting saloons, billiard halls, and gambling dens. Children made do with streets and vacant lots.

Even as the workers resisted, a growing cadre of upper- and middle-class civic reformers selectively attended to different aspects of social distress and environmental damage. These reformers included advocates such as Jane Addams, sympathetic to the plight of immigrant labor, who proposed physical improvements to the urban places where these people lived, which would re-create and restore the humanity lost to labor. Some focused on the housing stock, while others focused on parks that included fields, gardens, greens, ponds, and fountains that offered places for repose and recreation. Others embraced a top-down civic benevolence that envisioned the provision of public places for the working masses that would civilize the unkempt and unclean. The compassionate and benevolent activists fueled what was the Progressive reform movement, which included the provision of public improvements dedicated to improving the plight of the working classes while generating wholesome, beautiful places that everyone would enjoy.

The reformers set in motion institutional changes that stimulated public support for specialized public places and facilities designed to remedy urban ills, improve public health, foster recreation, and inspire civic uplift. I offer only a few highlights of the many initiatives that emerged in the late nineteenth and early twentieth centuries to remedy the excesses of industrial urbanization and laid the infrastructure for play.

Large urban parks provided pastoral open spaces surrounded and populated by stands of trees, ponds, fountains, field houses, meeting halls, gardens, and playing fields. Smaller specialized parks scattered across neighborhoods provided playgrounds, fields for sports, and landscaped paths for strolling. Parks offered places for protection and recovery from the physical ills of the industrial city. Public health initiatives focused on improving hygiene for adults and the development of children through the provision of public baths and dedicated playgrounds. Supporters of the playground movement hoped not only to improve the safety for child play but also to contribute to improved learning and moral health.

Municipalities funded and provided space for parks in response to the dramatic expansion of industrial cities. They offered an antidote to urban ills, a place for active recreation, a vehicle for public hygiene, and a resource for civic identity.[1] The pastoral landscape created by the English gentry was transformed into an urbanized nature by nineteenth-century landscape planners such as Frederick Law Olmsted, whose Central Park offered a regional park that met all of these goals. Best of all, for the champions of real estate, proximity to parkland offered a resale premium. The land adjoining Central Park enjoys much higher value than similar parcels just a few blocks away. Integrating nature into the spatial fabric of prosperous residential communities followed the class contours set by the rural gentry, merging the pastoral landscape with the myth of the yeoman farmstead, fueling the dream of a single-family home in a garden. Developers produced these places for prosperous upper- and middle-class households. But what about the growing crowds of people squeezed into the tenement districts of industrial cities like Chicago?

Reformers envisioned the provision of places dedicated exclusively for different kinds of play, and state legislatures created park districts for that purpose. Initially, these efforts continued to expand the provision of regional parks that catered to suburban elites and new middle-class home owners. Radical planning reformers such as Ebenezer Howard envisioned garden cities constructed on the suburban periphery that could tame the beast of industrial production and integrate the working-class residents within a garden landscape that unsettled the dominance of capitalist growth. Moderate reformers envisioned physical improvements that placed parkland and garden landscapes onto the underlying industrial system. Daniel Burnham's Chicago plan used parks and parkways to break up the massive grid and turn a squalid industrial lakefront into a pastoral parkway.

Museums, theaters, and concert halls were built for the entire city; these were large buildings, prominently positioned in accessible locations, to house events offering practical education and civic enlightenment for the public. The growing ranks of the urban and suburban middle class proved the most frequent users. The working classes showed up for periodic events but remained sequestered in low-rent districts using vacant and abandoned sites to play ball, picnic, and socialize. The working class frequented privately sponsored saloons, amusement parks, dance halls, gambling joints, burlesque clubs, and boxing arenas. The inexpensive availability of such places challenged the moral sensibilities of many reformers, who turned to the power of public regulations to spatially constrain and even outlaw these places. These efforts never completely succeeded, as working people resisted, and with their increasing participation in the electorate the norms for public activity expanded to include gambling and boxing.

City Beautiful proponents designed garden landscapes that used the spatial organization and location of plants, trees, and grass to cultivate places offering the experience of organic natural harmony to offset the excess of industrial urbanism. Reformers believed in public moral improvement through the tactile experience of natural environments tailored to the purposes of recreation and repose. Inspired by conceptions of civic unity, the practical effects of these improvements catered to the sensibilities of social elites and aspiring middle-class households. These civic-minded elites, confident in the powers of industrial might and national expansion, organized massive public fairs to celebrate the march of progress. The Crystal City concept first developed in London inspired the Columbian Exhibition in Chicago, designed by Burnham and Olmsted. The millions who visited the Chicago Columbian Exhibition walked the pastoral promenade, gazed upon the grand civic architecture, and peeked inside to witness the industrial tools on display. Once edified, they then escaped to the adjoining Midway for food, drink, entertainment, distraction, and play. The social differences separated and celebrated in the civic order of the White City coexisted as a riot of exotic juxtapositions among magicians, dancers, musicians, actors, and other players plying their trade among the promoters, hucksters, vendors, and assorted entrepreneurs selling food, drink, amusement, and more.

Play became not only a respite from toil but also an important contribution to human fulfillment and even citizenship. Jane Addams's Hull House used organized play not only for immigrant children but for adults as well. The successful provision of public schools provided an institutional beachhead for pragmatist-inspired pedagogical innovations that incorporated play into the mix of experiential learning. Doctrinal education began a long, strategic retreat that continues even to this day.

Increased prosperity among the urban working- and middle-class households made it possible to support the creation of public gymnasiums, professional sports teams, organized school-sponsored sport leagues, and intramural sports associations and the provision of public and private facilities, fields, and equipment. Playgrounds that were exceptional at the turn of the nineteenth century had by the end of the 1920s become routine spaces for elementary school yards and neighborhood parks.

THE NEW DEAL LEGACY AND CHICAGO AT MID-TWENTIETH CENTURY

The refinement of play into increasingly specialized arts, sports, and cultural activities incorporated the social inequalities of the marketplace and politics. Places for play were carved out in growing cities based on differences tied to social standing within class, race, and ethnic hierarchies. New Deal public works efforts included the construction of public facilities for play at an unprecedented scale. The federal initiative built on the efforts of Progressive reformers, labor unions, corporate managers, and social scientists studying leisure. Unemployed working-class workers built the physical infrastructure for play in urban and rural areas, while middle-class white-collar workers performed, taught, and promoted a diverse array of organized leisure activities. The Great Depression put a halt to urban expansion and the creation of new parks. But the New Deal's Works Progress Administration included recreational facilities as an important product of publicly funded construction work. Much of the funding went to improve national and state park facilities, but some ended up funding construction of park and recreational facilities in metropolitan regions such as Chicago.

Chicago mayor Anton Cermak, for instance, commissioned construction of the Grant Park band shell in 1931. In 1935 James C. Petrillo, president of the Chicago Federation of Musicians, convinced park district officials to launch a series of summer public concerts.[2] These events attracted tens of thousands of listeners who enjoyed the free entertainment provided by publicly funded musicians. This tradition continued until the 1950s, when television and suburban out-migration dampened demand for downtown gathering. It reawakened with Mayor Jane Byrne, who in 1981 opened Grant Park for a one-week food festival showcasing local restaurant fare while offering musical events and dance. A city office of cultural affairs sponsored events in public venues, such as public parks, buildings, plazas, and streets, throughout the year. These celebrations combined city funds with private philanthropy and volunteer efforts among citizens seeking places and venues for different types of play. The institutional infrastructure for cultural events planned and coordinated the physical use of public facilities and places across the urban landscape.

The New Deal efforts to preserve and celebrate regional culture offering publicly funded support for music, art, dance, and crafts proved short-lived and largely unnecessary in the boom years following World War II. Rising disposable income fueled the expansion of leisure into tourism and new forms of cultural consumption. Consider, for example, the Olympics. Revived in 1896 to inspire the celebration and promotion of amateur athletics (just as professional athletics was taking off), the modern Olympics links the sports competition with a different host city. The focus of the event remains amateur sport, but the economic and cultural impacts have shifted to emphasize the economic outcome and physical legacy of the public investment host cities make for local infrastructural improvements. In 1992 expenditures for the sporting events accounted for only 17 percent of total Olympic costs. In recent decades the International Olympic Committee has found it difficult to find cities in democratic societies willing and able to shoulder the burden of financial risk, as the public effect of Olympic legacies becomes less evident.

The opening of Disneyland in 1954 turned the garden-city dream of a beautiful place offering playful organic balance between town and country with home and work into an engineered park on a grand scale.[3] Walt Disney integrated what the Columbian Exhibition had separated: the edification of modern technology and the pleasing amusement of the midway carnival. Increased prosperity and mobility encouraged the proliferation of specialized places designed to attract visitors. The tourist industry advertised and promoted experiences unique to a specific locale. Las Vegas also came into its own as a destination for illicit adult play. Del Webb designed residential retirement communities as exclusive places for leisure and play for the elderly. Single-family suburban homes transforming urban landscapes across the United

States included increasingly sophisticated appliances, providing more time and space for leisure and play. The private purchase and use of toys, games, sports equipment, tools, craft accessories, and other leisure objects exploded.

The ubiquity of human play, like the ubiquity of the natural environment, succumbed to the clever and relentless penetration of market relations. Supermarkets and fast-food joints that offered plenty of popular, cheap food fifty years ago today pose a public health hazard. The popular embrace of toys and video games advertised on television and the Internet faces scrutiny today as people recognize how they distract children (and even adults) from active physical play. Massive cruise ships transport tourists to visit destinations where buses and trams shuttle thousands of visitors to popular but ill-prepared historical sites. Leisure as passive consumption of manufactured goods, services, and experiences has displaced active play. The results have not only damaged individuals but also generated enormous collective costs on places and society. Public health problems emerge (for example, diabetes) as obesity reaches epidemic proportions. Popular tourist destinations suffer physical decay and environmental pollution from excessive levels of use. The commodification of play has perhaps gone too far.

CONTEMPORARY DEMAND FOR PLAY

According to the U.S. Statistical Abstract, all areas of leisure experienced increased revenues between 2000 and 2010. Spectating accounts for the largest share. Attendance at sports and entertainment performances accounts for an increasing share of spectating, while museum and amusement-park attendance lags. Gambling dramatically increased its share of leisure revenue. Expenditures for active recreation overall diminished, even as revenues from fitness-center membership increased. Table 1 breaks down the industrial sectors showing revenue growth and the different rates over a seventeen-year interval.

Active and Passive Play among U.S. Adults

The demand for passive enjoyment of places and events outpaces purchases that involve active play. Despite the rapid increases in gambling and fitness revenue, revenue of other forms of active amusement lagged. Participation in spectating leads revenue growth in the leisure industry. This squares with data on attendance data for public parks. A third of the largest one hundred cities reported park-hosted events surpassing one hundred thousand attendees. Among the largest were San Diego's Fourth of July celebrations, Fort Worth's

Table 1. U.S. arts and entertainment employer revenue by subsector

Sectors	Growth rate (%) 1998–2015	Employment in millions		
		1998	2007	2015
Arts, entertainment, and recreation overall	1.11	128,290	215,705	272,324
Performing arts, spectator sports, and related	1.31	56,647	98,339	132,450
Museums, historical sites, and similar	0.87	8,356	13,384	15,297
Amusement, gambling, and recreational industries	0.92	63,287	103,982	124,595

Source: U.S. Census Bureau, "Service Annual Survey Historical Data (NAICS Basis), 2015," table 1, https://census.gov/data/tables/2015/econ/services/sas-naics.html.

Mayfest, the Oklahoma City Spring Arts Festival, the Taste of Chicago, and San Francisco's Hardly Strictly Bluegrass Festival.[1]

The 2013 U.S. Statistical Abstract reports on a 2010 national survey detailing what adults do in their leisure time. Away-from-home activities overwhelmingly included passive spectator attendance at performances and sporting events. A few, like playing a musical instrument or chess, could happen in a public place, but most play people reported doing happened at home. Missing altogether was mention of participation in sports, fitness-related activities, or other forms of social group activity. More recent data from the annual time survey conducted by the U.S. Bureau of Labor Statistics shows that among all people fifteen years or older, leisure and sports activity accounts for about 5 hours a day. Most of this included sedentary activity: people on average spend 2 hours and 43 minutes watching television, 19 minutes relaxing and thinking, 17 minutes reading, 14 minutes gaming, 10 minutes on the computer, 4 minutes on arts, 40 minutes socializing, and 2 minutes watching sporting events. This left 19 minutes for active sports play and exercise. Most adults do little or no active play. Among the 21 percent who do, the average was about 90 minutes of active sport or exercise (mostly walking) per day. Surprisingly, adults work for only 3 hours and 36 minutes and spend 1 hour and 10 minutes traveling—most sitting in cars.[5] A comparison with 2006 data revealed very little change over time.

There is some evidence that working adults spend more leisure time in motion. A recent study collected data for U.S. workers in the National Health Interview Survey. Leisure-time physical activity was categorized as sufficiently active (moderate intensity, 150 minutes per week), insufficiently active (10–149 minutes per week), and inactive (less than 10 minutes per week).

Prevalence trends of "sufficient" LTPA significantly increased from 2004 to 2014 (45.6 percent to 54.8 percent; $P < .001$).[6]

Children and Play

A report prepared by the National Physical Activity Plan Alliance in 2016 details youth activity levels across the United States. The report compiles survey results from several national data sources. They report that in 2005–6 about 43 percent of children six to eleven years old were physically active 50 minutes a day for five days of a week, while only 8 percent of middle school and 5 percent of high school students reported meeting that standard. Sedentary activity was prevalent among all three, but highest among teens, 70 percent of whom reported spending more than 2 hours a day watching a screen.

Schools play a prominent role shaping not only what children learn but how they do it. Nine of ten elementary schools continue to provide recess for children, although many fewer offer formal physical education classes. About half the adolescents in the United States attend at least one PE class a week.

The U.S. Department of Health and Human Services set out to track physical activity for all people, including children. They started tracking elementary and secondary school support for physical education as part of increased attention to active play as an important contribution to improved public health. The results showed some increasing efforts by districts across the United States to require physical education but at very small percentage values. Elementary

Table 2. U.S. Department of Health and Human Services, increases in share of physical activity in schools

| | Actual years | | | Goal |
	2000	2006	2014	2020
Increased share of elementary schools requiring daily PE		4.4	3.6	4.8
Increased share of junior high schools requiring daily PE		10.5	3.3	11.5
Increased share of high schools requiring daily PE	5.8	2.1	4.0	2.3
Increased share of adolescent daily participation		30.0	30.0	37.0
Increased share of districts requiring elementary recess		57.0	59.0	63.0
Increased share of districts that allow physical activity use after school	35.0	29.0	26.0	32.0

Source: U.S. Department of Health and Human Services, *Healthy People, 2020*, Office of Disease Prevention and Health Promotion, 2017, https://www.healthypeople.gov/2020/default.

schools are increasing required recess even as they are proving less generous in sharing facilities for physical activity after school hours.

Demand for active play has increased among adults and for small children in recent years. However, people spend more time alone engaging in mostly private at-home sedentary activity. More households have increased spending on spectator activities than spend time and money on active play with others.

Private provision currently dominates the infrastructure for play. This reflects the prosperity of the U.S. economy and the cultural focus on independence and autonomy. A robust leisure industry has grown and diversified, developing ways to fill adult leisure time with profitable pursuits. Mostly these include products, places, and events that entertain and amuse. The promotion and production of fitness have fueled expansion in health clubs and exercise gear, but mostly for niche segments.

EMERGING PROBLEMS FOR PLAY

Play accompanies childhood and contributes to learning the practical arts of adult living. Play happens as part of social and spatial settings. Play embeds each developing child within a nexus of traditions, habits, and techniques encountered as simulations, models, and tools for understanding, manipulating, and otherwise conceiving the world. Play not only integrates children into a household, neighborhood, and society but also provides the ensemble of tacit skills for self-development. The promise of modernity anticipates the provision of social and political freedom sufficient to support the continued articulation of each person. Each person must learn to become a responsible individual, able to integrate the multiple roles of worker, parent, citizen, and more. This proves difficult to do in finding a role in the labor market, creating a family, maintaining a home, caring for kin, and the other demands of independent adulthood. Play provides crucial experience for learning how to manage and juggle these roles into a coherent self.[7]

Making places for play that can meet this challenge fueled the ambitions of civic reformers more than a century ago and continues to inspire the efforts of those building pathways to human fulfillment that make room for play. Private provision currently dominates the infrastructure for play. This reflects the prosperity of the U.S. economy and the cultural focus on independence and autonomy. A robust leisure industry has identified and exploited spatial niches for consumption accelerated and complemented by Internet communication and interaction. But market infrastructure for play also contributes to problems that the market cannot solve.

Social Differences Generate Uneven Access and Use

The diversity, depth, and range of places for play vary with the class, gender, and age of people. The sweeping egalitarian impulses that inspired the reformers a hundred years ago had to adapt to the demands and expectations of elite institutions and expectations. The basic playgrounds that became standard fare for public schools were no match for the expansive grounds at elite private schools. The recognition of child's play as serious business enriched the manufacture of mass-produced playground equipment purchased by school districts and municipalities, even as park districts in wealthy areas provided hand-crafted private and semipublic playgrounds and recreational facilities.

Looked at in the aggregate, the United States possesses an astonishing amount of public and private places for play. But the class disparities that diminished in the wake of the Great Depression have returned. The privatization of professional sports, the expanded popularity of gambling as a source of public revenue, the sprawling growth of exclusive and unsustainable golf courses, the popularity of computer gaming, and social media have channeled play into places that marginalize, exploit, and exclude people based on differences in income, race, ethnicity, age, religion, and gender.

This segmentation does not flow inevitably from the availability of increased time, new technologies, digital communication, or other specialized tools for playing. In fact, the innovations offer new opportunities for enhancing and improving the possibilities for active interactive play that cuts across market and social divides. This requires purposeful effort and attention.

Sedentary Living and High-Calorie Diets Generate Chronic Health Risks

The success of modern employment, housing, and transportation systems has greatly reduced our reliance on physical activity. People spend more time sitting than moving as they do their jobs, traveling among destinations, and living in their homes. Chronic illnesses and health risks once kept in check by the physical effort expended by making things, walking to work, and actively maintaining a home have increased. Additionally, people enjoy access to more inexpensive food, much of it laced with high-calorie sugar and fat that encourage addiction. These emerging health risks fall disproportionately across the population based on cultural eating habits and income level. The food industry's advertising caters to paying clientele based on cultural tastes and buying power. Poor people purchase and eat familiar, affordable high-calorie, low-nutrition food and drink that wealthier people generally do not eat. The incidence rates for obesity and diabetes that headline public health campaigns reach epidemic levels in poor neighborhoods. Changing what people eat and how they move becomes a target for publicly fostered reform. For instance, advocates have urged retail supermarket firms to locate stores in food deserts. We must ask what sorts of institutional and physical changes would improve the infrastructure for active physical play.

Seeing Instead of Doing

Municipalities, park districts, tourist bureaus, and other event planners build infrastructure that encourages large-scale spectator events. Sports arenas and racetracks offer examples of publicly subsidized, privately managed places for popular professional teams tied to a region or city. Hosting the Olympic Games represents the pinnacle of massive publicly subsidized sports infra-structure provision. Across the globe, municipalities and their national governments compete to attract the Games and usually spend a decade building and improving facilities in a metropolitan region. The competition among elite amateur (sort of) athletes from across the globe attracts millions of visitors who offer billions of tourist dollars to the host country. The promised residual benefits of the construction funded by speculators and lenders rarely materialize. Millions of people watch and enjoy the competition as spectators and consumers eating, drinking, shopping, and touring.

Daniel Burnham and Edward Bennett's famous 1909 *Plan of Chicago* was initially conceived as an expansive lakefront park inspired while preparing for the Columbian Exhibition in the 1890s. Burnham was a civic booster who believed that public provision of beautiful parkways, plazas, and parks would create places that not only eased congestion and stimulated invest-ment but also housed civic spectacles inspiring solidarity and pride. The museum campus near the massively rebuilt Chicago Bears football stadium was a catalyst for the reconfiguration of a large portion of Lakefront Drive and Roosevelt Road in the 1990s. The ensuing realignment opened up the South Side of the Loop for redevelopment while increasing access to these regional attractions.

The Chicago culture campus offers an excellent example of the tension between the passive spectacle of museum display and professional sports against the active engagement of public amateurs playing ball and hiking in a nature preserve. The campus improvements proved so successful that the site attracted the attention of George Lucas, whose real estate team was scouting locations outside California for a museum showcasing and celebrating his epic moviemaking enterprise. Chicago's "Friends of the Parks" successfully sued the Chicago Park District, arguing that the private museum should not locate in prime public trust parkland adjacent to Lake Michigan. Discouraged by the legal impediments and uninterested in other less prominent Chicago sites, Lucas dropped the proposal. Much less contentious was the creation of the First Merit Bank concert pavilion on the northern half of Northerly Island (formerly Meigs Field), which generated ticket-sale revenue that the park district used to help pay for the reclamation of the ninety-two-acre peninsula as a pedestrian- and bicycle-friendly nature preserve that combines seeing and doing.

Gambling to the Rescue

The Las Vegas Strip provides the consummate example of an urban space designed for mass leisure. Visitors travel from across the globe to gamble and periodically attend large-scale entertainment events when otherwise not eating and drinking. Once reviled as a place of immorality and crime, Las Vegas became a role model for public leisure. In the past fifty years states have approved casino gambling and statewide lotteries that generate substantial revenue for the state. Indian tribes entered the business as well, creating casinos on reservations close to highways and near metropolitan areas. Legalizing and taxing gambling does not remedy the addictive features of gambling, which makes it a controversial form of play. One 2002 study found that 80 percent of adults gambled at least once in the prior year.[8]

Exurban postindustrial suburbs encircling Chicago have built riverboat casinos, taxing the gaming revenues to support redevelopment in obsolete downtowns. The expected multiplier effects did not materialize as many hoped, and the social costs remain untallied. Gambling has spread to online video gaming, greatly decentralizing digital access to games of chance. A 2015 report by the video (gambling) gaming industry uses Illinois gaming tax-revenue flows to document how casino revenues are declining, while revenues from machines located in almost a thousand Illinois municipalities accounted for 28 percent of the state's gambling revenue in 2014.[9] Ironically, promoting gambling as a revenue source promotes forms of leisure-time activity that foster types of play that do little to contribute to improved health or meaningful fulfillment.

States, municipalities, counties, and special-district authorities promote projects (for example, stadia) and policies (such as gambling) that encourage tourist and hospitality activity to expand growth in the postindustrial service sector, fueling both economic growth and public revenues. These efforts contribute to problem play. Other public agencies, but sometimes the same ones, build and support infrastructure for play that struggles to promote active forms of play to improve public health and support the growth and development of individuals.

SUPPLYING PUBLIC INFRASTRUCTURE FOR PLAY

Local park provision proliferated in the early twentieth century as a functional department within municipal (and urban county) bureaucracies. These departments provide the primary public infrastructure for play across the United States. Their efforts are complemented by elementary and secondary school districts. School districts concentrate on education in classrooms and laboratories, but they also provide an astonishing range of facilities and structures for informal and formal play. Today both offer passive and active places for play. The playground equipment and sports equipment industries now help fund and promote the public agencies that continue to champion public parks and playgrounds.

Parks

The Trust for Public Land collected data on public parkland in the one hundred largest cities in the United States for 2015. The 2016 report identified 22,493 city parks serving 62 million urban residents with a wide array of facilities, including 419 public golf courses, 569 dog parks, 9,633 ball diamonds, 11,678 playgrounds, and 14,415 basketball hoops. A survey of park and recreational agencies of all sizes across the country uncovers an even larger network of park provision in suburbs, exurban, and rural communities.[10] The median agency administered 25 facilities on 491 acres. Playgrounds, courts, and fields were the most common facilities.

Park districts provide the primary public institution offering infrastructure for play. Like school districts, most park districts obtain operating revenue from property taxes. This introduces disparities across a metropolitan region. Districts that encompass prosperous communities can fund more and better facilities than those located in poor communities. The uneven funding of place-based taxation generates disparities in local access to facilities for play. Additionally, upper- and middle-class households enjoy more leisure time than working-class and poor households. They mobilize and leverage access and use of public district facilities and programs, coordinating a wide range of child-focused events. Indoor facilities were less common, but the most popular included recreational centers and gyms.

Schools

The creation of public schools in the United States laid down a powerful institutional infrastructure for human education and improvement. Elite reformers convinced reluctant peers that educating all citizens would improve not only the quality of labor but also the political strength of the democratic republic. The efforts to promote playgrounds started out independent of the schools but became part of the civic improvement reforms promoted by progressive reformers at the outset of the twentieth century. The idea that play contributes to improved learning remains to this day contested.

Public education has focused on teaching students to read, write, calculate, and acquire the basic rudiments of American civic culture and history. Many progressive reformers promoted developmental conceptions of childhood that integrated play into organized education—ideas that later social and psychological research refined and elaborated. But while these inspired innovations in private education and specialized curricula mostly for prosperous middle-class families, the public systems continued to separate play on the grounds from learning in the classrooms.

The performing and plastic arts along with sports did become an increasing part of school experience throughout the twentieth century. As school districts consolidated, they were able to build school facilities that included places for formal play: theaters, studios, stadia, pools, arenas, fields, and halls. Learning to play a musical instrument or baseball, swim, or draw was ancillary or secondary to the basic curriculum and the commitment to preparing students for the labor market. The cultural organization of play happened as parents with the financial support of business and civic sponsors created theater groups, sports leagues, and other specialized entities to solicit and promote participation. These spaces offered children opportunities to acquire and develop skills in different forms of play.

For more than a century, local public schools have organized play to fit purposefully into designed playgrounds, theaters, and gyms. The consolidated urban and suburban school districts build schools that include places to learn arts and sports. The same spatial segmentation of classroom work and play accompanied secondary school organization, but with larger and more specialized grounds and spaces, including fields, courts, and pools for informal play and formal games and sport. Today, students may elect to learn a musical instrument in band, play a specialized position on a sport team, create artistic drawings, or perform onstage as a dancer, singer, or actor, or perhaps all three. Each school or school district routinely provides places for the formal and informal conduct of such play.[11]

The connection between play, learning, and overall health continues to gain scientific and public support. But finding the resources to provide facilities for all students remains a challenge. The increasing residential segregation by income, race, and ethnic affiliation shows up in the local spatial organization of districts. Big-city districts face large portions of low-income minority students with shrinking property-tax bases. The surrounding metro suburban districts fare much better. These disparities can make an emerging public health problem like the obesity epidemic among youth much more challenging to prevent. As families eat tasty but nutritiously suspect processed food, those with lower incomes make such foods a larger part of their daily diet. Sugar- and fat-laden foods prove addictive to many. High-calorie, low-nutrition diets fuel fat formation unless offset by increased levels of physical activity. Public health advocates urge schools to offer more nutritious food and to encourage more physical activity during the school day. Play not only complements mental learning but also contributes crucially to physical health threatened by the addictive allure of junk food.

PAVING PATHWAYS FOR PLAY IN CHICAGO

The Chicago Park District

The Chicago Park District conducted a study of the economic impact that the district assets had on the city's economy for 2013. The impacts included direct effects tied to revenues from park-hosted events and the indirect impacts on the value of property near each type of park. The large magnet parks like Grant and Lincoln Parks along the lakefront provided the most direct revenue from tourism, while the other large regional, community, and neighborhood parks accounted for revenue from sponsored events.

Table 3. Parks' impact on property value

Park type	Count	Property value impact[a]	Special assets and tourism[a]	Nontax revenues[a]	Enrollment[b] (number of people)	Average property value impact (%)
Magnet	7	134	1,173–1,384	69	30,731	1.6
Mini	141	335	—	0	492	2.8
Neighborhood	161	146	20	1	74,084	0.9
Community	117	68	—	7	215,217	0.6
Regional	46	43	—	5	164,938	0.9
Citywide	9	9	10	3	41,227	0.8
Passive	56	159	—	0	13,548	2.4
Unimproved	21	13	—	—	—	0.8
Nature preserve	3	2.6	—	—	—	2.0
Total	557	909.6	1,180–1,391	86	540,237	1.5

Source: Chicago Park District, *The Power of Parks: An Assessment of Chicago Park's Economic Impact* (Chicago: Chicago Park District, 2014). Original source material contains mathematical errors, as reproduced here.
[a] In millions of dollars.
[b] Program and event enrollment.

The park district promotes events and programs that directly touch a half-million people each year. But most visits to local parks and the activities in which people engage remain unreported. People walk their dogs in and around these parks and children play on the grounds, but the total park space per person remains relatively low in many residential neighborhoods. Visiting parks and contact with nature are associated with improved physical and mental health,[12] including lower levels of obesity,[13] reduced stress,[14] positive moods and psychological well-being,[15] and positive feelings about place.[16]

Chicago Public Schools

Chicago's public schools, located across the city, offer grounds for children to play on for recess and physical education. However, much of the space provided for such activity has changed over time. Recess was eliminated to ensure more time was spent on academic instruction. PE classes were curtailed or eliminated. The playground space deteriorated or was covered with asphalt for parking or other uses. Additionally, the out-migration of many African American households from troubled inner-city neighborhoods and the influx of Latino households into other improving neighborhoods have put Chicago's public schools in a bind. Closing the low-enrollment elementary and secondary schools in poor African American neighborhoods removes an important local resource, while expanding and building new facilities in Latino areas generate resentment. Undertaking efforts to use school grounds for more active play requires money and attention that the school system cannot spare. But activists do not let that stop them.

The Spaces to Grow initiative was conceived to help revitalize school grounds. First, the effort recognizes and supports the crucial role that active physical play contributes to student learning and health. Second, the initiative recognizes the need for green areas to absorb rainwater in a city vulnerable to increased flooding. Third, many of these schools exist in low-income minority areas where children face increased risks for obesity and diabetes, conditions that increased physical activity can diminish. Finally, these improved places offer additional playground park space, improving access for underserved neighborhoods. The Spaces to Grow initiative is sponsored by several local government agencies (the public school system, the Metropolitan Water District, the Chicago Department of Water Management), the not-for-profit environmental organization Openlands, and the health advocacy organization Healthy Schools Campaign.

Parks and schools remain the two primary public institutions responsible for play that can still provide practical hopes for the ideals of civic improvement through the practical support of individual development. Modest resources and shifting priorities have meant that efforts to improve facilities and programs for play require collaboration among many agencies and actors. But the collaboration cannot rely on privatization; instead, it must include purposeful strategies that ensure that private involvement serves meaningful civic goals.

Conceiving the Future Infrastructure for Play in Chicago

Chicago has taken efforts over the years to build places for play. Any strategy for future improvement must build on these prior efforts. The 2012 Cultural Plan for Chicago includes three primary objectives that implicitly recognize the contribution that serious human play makes to the culture of the city and society:

1. make beautiful objects, events, and experiences that shape and express local identity and solidarity
2. inspire innovative adaptive reuse for ordinary or obsolete places and things
3. create and celebrate culturally distinct art, dance, food, and landscapes

These plan objectives step around the deep class and ethnic divisions that persist in the segregation of housing and schools. The ambitious list taps the long history of progressive reform that tries to use the purposeful design of places to respond to larger social divisions and conflicts. The popular conception of creative cities often focuses too narrowly on a few prosperous elite neighborhoods near downtown. This misses how the play people manage to conduct across the intrusion of cultural difference, social inequality, and spatial complexity fuels creative possibilities. Violence, ignorance, subjection, discrimination, and other forms of destructive social conduct do not foster creativity. But many people who inhabit places where these conditions persist use practical cultural inheritance to weave family, food, friendship, and worship into crucibles for creativity despite the obstacles. Current efforts to improve and expand the urban infrastructure for play can adopt the objectives of the cultural plan to recognize and guide important improvement.

FILL SPACES WITH BEAUTIFUL PLACES   Tourism integrates institutional and physical infrastructure to attract and manage increasing flows of strangers who visit and experience sites and events in prepared venues. Theme parks planned, constructed, and managed by private corporations now provide iconic places. Walt Disney, influenced by garden-city plans, conceived theme parks that integrated specialized landscapes as vicarious experiences scripted for mass consumption. He used the powers of modern engineering to bind together places for exhibition with places for amusement into thematic landscapes. These places combine ideas from garden-city enthusiasts, park designers, civil engineers, entertainment providers, and land developers. Disney developed and implemented alternative transit systems to move people across and around the park. Linking entertainment with functional movement made transit travel pleasant and so a more plausible alternative for travel in Tomorrow Land.

Many theme parks do not offer the quality of integration that Disney set in motion. These planned places offer thematic amusements, especially rides on large mechanical devices designed to offer extraordinary physical sensations of speed, dizziness, weightlessness, and disorientation. The fun and distraction of amusement for the most part take visitors for a ride. They do not foster the kind of play that the public health advocates hope to encourage.

Municipalities coordinate with tourist bureaus to attract visitors to public stadia, theaters, and museums. The development of large regional parks can be undertaken to attract visitors. Chicago's Millennium Park, completed in 2004, offers a prominent example of a large-scale project that, despite its expense and location on a huge underground parking structure, offered a central place for active and passive play.

Millennium Park beautifully balances the powers of spectacle and pedestrian pleasure. Set back to midblock, the hall and stage anchor rather than dominate the park campus. The adjoining garden, field, and Maggie Daley Children's Park offer places for restful repose and lively interaction, splashing in the shallow fountains, peering at contorted reflections of skyscrapers reflected on the massive bean, ogling a multitude of flowering plants, or exploring the playground. This uniquely urban place for play remains tied to the demands of suburban automobile access. The costly underground parking garage meant that public financing was insufficient and private philanthropy substantial. The donors enjoy prominent plaques and monuments memorializing their contributions throughout the park.

The park district struggles to maintain the existing parks, with the smallest parks receiving the least attention and revenue. The district has adopted art and music programs that sponsor events in the larger parks and host annual events in the largest. The parks include hundreds of sculptures and fountains. A 2014 report documented the successful impact that large magnet parks contribute to tourist revenue and to local land values in nearby residential neighborhoods. But the crucial impact of parks as places for active play remains significant, with room for growth.[17]

INSPIRE ADAPTIVE REUSE   Harnik and Bloomberg detail the kinds of places where parks might find a toehold in cities: landfills, wetlands, rail trails, wetlands and stream corridors, cemeteries, boulevards, and even little-traveled streets or the parking spaces on those streets. Chicago has already capitalized on two natural and man-made corridors.[18]

The early environmental plans for the Chicago River, for instance, focused on water quality—reducing decades of industrial and residential pollution. The river had become a conduit for waste. The meandering streams that fed marshland hosting a vast diversity of wildlife two hundred years ago were systematically channeled into a single stream for increasing quantities of effluent. The massive and rapid growth in population and industry at the end of the nineteenth and in the early twentieth centuries spurred efforts for improved infrastructure. Three massive channeling efforts between the 1890s and the 1920s successfully altered the river flow away from Lake Michigan to the Mississippi River. Tapping the Great Lakes to flush away polluted water raised political opposition from people living in the other states and provinces adjoining the Great Lakes. Legal battles ended with an international agreement enabling Chicago to use water from the Great Lakes, but with annual limits imposed and the requirement that the water be treated to reduce pollution before launching it downstream. The quality remained industrial grade until the 1960s, when Chicago's water-polluting industrial industries folded, moved away, or downsized to meet the shifting demands of an increasing global economy. Environmental activity by activists and water-quality policies promoted by the newly fashioned Environmental Protection Agency reclaimed the river for lost ecological and recreational use. This quest has taken decades of purposeful collaborative efforts by advocacy organizations (Friends of the Chicago River), government agencies (the City of Chicago, Metropolitan Water Reclamation District, EPA), and the courts. Plans created in the 1990s and 2000s not only ensure the continued flow of shipping but also take important steps in infrastructural improvement to make places for active recreation. The river provides a physical pathway through increasingly obsolete industrial land, offering an opportunity for creative mixed-use development that includes places for walking, cycling, and water-related recreation.

Another more recent example is the recovery of an abandoned railway right-of-way. The 606 runs along Bloomingdale Avenue on Chicago's northwest side, connecting the nearby neighborhoods of Logan Square, Humboldt Park, Wicker Park, and Bucktown, as well as the Chicago River and several city boulevards. Its centerpiece is the elevated 2.7-mile Bloomingdale Trail, built on the unused Bloomingdale railroad. The 606 will ultimately comprise the trail, six neighborhood parks, a public plaza, an observatory, art installations, educational programming, and other amenities. "The 606 not only serves nearby neighborhoods, but also provides a way for people from across the city and region to explore these diverse and culturally rich neighborhoods," said Chicago Park District superintendent Mike Kelly. "It advances the green vision of Daniel Burnham's 1909 Plan of Chicago."

In 2003 neighborhood residents and activists established Friends of the Bloomingdale Trail to introduce and advance the concept of the trail. They approached the Trust for Public Land about building a park along the western end of the trail; Julia de Burgos Park, the first of five new parks that are part of the 606, was developed on that site by the Trust for Public Land and Chicago Park District in 2008. Mayor Rahm Emanuel made the 606 (after Chicago's zip code prefix) a signature project for his effort to create new parks, recreation areas, and green spaces throughout Chicago. It opened to the public in June 2015. The park not only transformed a hulking, obsolete rail embankment into a green corridor but also activated the improved pathway for active cycling, walking, and jogging, integrating parks and semipublic open spaces into places for play. Other rail embankments exist but in less prosperous neighborhoods, where efforts to revitalize will require a wider scope and stronger nodes attracting and connecting walkers, runners, and cyclists.

CREATE PLACES THAT EMBRACE DIVERSITY   Our expectations for play often distract us from the extraordinary adaptability that we may each deploy in its service. The social conventions separating work and play discourage blending the two. Those of us accessing jobs as professionals, managers, and executives can study and nurture elements of play to enhance our work, while those making, selling, and servicing products must keep both apart. Supervisors insist employees concentrate on the work and avoid the distraction of play. The conventions that segment labor and housing markets carry over into how and where people play. But cities can design and make places that increase the opportunity for interaction across these divides.

The large regional magnet parks provide places that the city can use to host annual events celebrating music (the jazz festival, blues concerts, world music), dance (salsa, ballroom), and cuisine (Taste of Chicago), attracting people from every class, race, and ethnic group. The success has translated into neighborhood-scale events that celebrate aspects of local culture, attracting visitors to join with locals in play that enables people to share the pleasures of unfamiliar differences. The city takes steps to coordinate, promote, and subsidize these events across many different neighborhoods.

The lopsided development that has accompanied land development in aging, racially segmented cities like Chicago creates unfavorable conditions for greening the thousands of vacant parcels that accompany the depopulation of African American inner-city neighborhoods.[19] The demand for parks follows the contours of increased density. Community gardens and other local experiments converting empty parcels into places for active use and play provide islands of innovation rather than seeds propagating a revitalized system.

CONCLUSION

Ultimately, almost anything or any place in the world may offer infrastructure for human play. The most hopeful aspects of local agency involvement with play come from examples of collaborative effort that revise the tradition of civic involvement. Chicago has taken important steps in the past twenty years to improve and revitalize its largest parks. The challenge of activating the smaller parks into a system linked with school grounds and other potential local spaces for play remains. Making parks and school grounds multipurpose, integrating ecological infrastructure with fields and grounds that invite active play, and weaving healthy activities with the pleasures of play will take resources that the park district and school district do not possess.

How Play Might Matter in the Long Run

Accelerated digital automation across the globe promises to transform the fossil fuel–based industrial labor economy into a renewable energy–based information economy. Agricultural innovations and changes that foster sustainable, quality food provision will reduce reliance on subsistence and illicit farming practices. Continued urban migration will lead to improved literacy and education for women. As fertility levels decline and become stable, economic growth will rely almost entirely on the value added by human education and innovation. The meaning of work will shift from just a special kind of commodity to being allocated within local markets to a more complex set of practical skills, ideas, codes, and conventions that channel and mediate markets for private, common, and public goods across places. These changes are happening across vast segments of industry but remain tied to conventions of political and social control that resist change.

Imagine leisure and play no longer treated as escapes from the exploitation and drudgery of labor but as activities integrated into daily life as the norm. Recess is not escape from boring rote learning. School includes observing and reporting on the behavior of insect colonies in a nearby field, learning how to dance and sing about feelings, using tools to fix broken objects, and doing other activities that integrate the pleasure of discovery through movement with the discipline of science, literature, language, and arts and crafts. The developmental dreams of early-twentieth-century progressive education reformers challenged the necessity of economic and cultural segmentation and exclusion. The creative power of play in this urban future taps and develops practical forms of diverse knowledge and experience to foster individual flourishing. The legacies of repression and exploitation remain but are no longer justified as necessary and inevitable. The feast of fools overwhelms the unheavenly city.[20]

Notes

1. R. F. Bachin, "Cultivating Unity: The Changing Role of Parks in Urban America," *Places* 15, no. 3 (2003): 12–17.

2. Dennis H. Cremin, *Developing Grant Park: The Evolution of Chicago's Front Yard* (Carbondale: Southern Illinois University Press, 2014), 127–29.

3. Disney had grand urban design ambitions for what later become Epcot Center. He had no inkling of the irony that his development success had wrought.

4. Trust for Public Land 2011, "2011 City Park Facts," Center for Park Excellence, https://www.tpl.org/2011-city-park-facts-report-0#sm.0001rxahektdkf94q4y2ipcowzkvz.

5. Forty-five percent of the adults reported working on average eight hours per day.

6. Ja K. Gu et al., "Prevalence and Trends of Leisure-Time Physical Activity by Occupation and Industry in U.S. Workers: The National Health Interview Survey, 2004–2014," *Annals of Epidemiology* 26, no. 10 (2016): 685–92.

7. Elizabeth Goodenough, ed., *A Place for Play: A Companion Volume to the Michigan Television Film "Where Do the Children Play?"* (Carmel Valley, CA: National Institute for Play, 2008).

8. J. W. Welte, "Gambling Participation in the U.S.: Results from a National Survey," *Journal of Gambling Studies* 18, no. 4 (2002): 313–37, doi:10.1023/A:1021019915591.

9. Union Gaming Analytics, "Illinois Gaming Machine Operators Association: Economic Impact Study Final Report," 2015, http://igmoa.org/wp-content/uploads/2015/03/UGA-IGMOA-Economic-Impact-Study_FINAL-short-form-released.pdf.

10. National Recreation and Park Association, "NRPA Agency Performance Review: Park and Recreation Agency Performance Benchmarks, 2017," 2017, http://www.nrpa.org/siteassets/nrpa-agency-performance-review.pdf.

11. The research evidence on child play at school supports the provision of physical facilities for active movement, even as some of these may be more useful than others. Brendon Hyndman, A. Benson, and A. Teleford, "Active Play: Exploring the Influences on Children's School Playground Activities," *American Journal of Play* 8, no. 3 (2016).

12. Andrew Mowen et al., "The Role of Park Proximity and Social Support in Shaping Park Visitation, Physical Activity, and Perceived Health among Older Adults," *Journal of Physical Activity and Health* 4, no. 2 (2007): 167–79; K. A. Shores and S. T. West, "The Relationship between Built Park Environments and Physical Activity in Four Park Locations," *Journal of Public Health Management & Practice* 14, no. 3 (2008): 9–16.

13. K. Lachowycz and A. P. Jones, "Greenspace and Obesity: A Systematic Review of the Evidence," *Obesity Reviews* 12 (2011): e183–e189.

14. Laura L. Payne et al., "Local Park Use and Personal Health among Older Adults: An Exploratory Study," *Journal of Park and Recreation Administration* 23, no. 2 (2005): 1–20.

15. P. H. Gobster and L. M. Westphal, "The Human Dimensions of Urban Greenways: Planning for Recreation and Related Experiences," *Landscape and Urban Planning* 68 (2004): 147–65.

16. K. Tzoulas et al., "Promoting Ecosystem and Human Health in Urban Areas Using Green Infrastructure: A Literature Review," *Landscape and Urban Planning* 81, no. 3 (2001): 167–78; Julie K. Clark and Taylor V. Stein, "Incorporating the Natural Landscape within an Assessment of Community Attachment," *Forest Science* 49, no. 6 (2003): 867–76.

17. *The Power of Parks: An Assessment of Chicago Parks' Economic Impact* (Chicago: Chicago Park District, 2014).

18. Peter Harnik and Mayor Michael Bloomberg, *Urban Green: Innovative Parks for Resurgent Cities* (Washington, DC: Island Press, 2014).

19. J. Schilling and J. Logan, "Greening the Rust Belt: A Green Infrastructure Model for Right Sizing America's Shrinking Cities," *Journal of the American Planning Association* 74, no. 4 (2008): 451–66.

20. Harvey Cox, *The Feast of Fools: A Theological Essay on Festivity and Fantasy* (Cambridge, MA: Harvard University Press, 1969); Edward Banfield, *The Unheavenly City* (New York: Little, Brown, 1970).

Planning and Financing Infrastructure in the Trump Years

What Can the Administration Learn from Previous Large Infrastructure Programs?

BEVERLY BUNCH

In June 2017, President Donald Trump released a $1 trillion infrastructure plan to rebuild America's infrastructure. Although specific provisions were not released at that time, the plan proposes to decrease the average permit time from ten years to two years, to "unleash private sector capital and expertise to rebuild our cities and states," to invest in rural infrastructure, to "reimagine America's approach to infrastructure with transformative projects," and to initiate workforce training focused on skills-based apprenticeship education.[1]

The plan proposes $200 billion in federal funding for infrastructure projects, including $25 billion for rural infrastructure, $15 billion for transformative projects, and $100 billion for local prioritization of infrastructure needs. The $200 billion is intended to leverage additional funds, which would result in a total infrastructure investment of $1 trillion. The plan also calls for one million apprentices within two years. The White House describes the "Rebuild America" infrastructure plan as a major component of President Trump's agenda to promote job creation and economic growth.

To help inform the current debate on how to address the nation's infrastructure, this chapter examines three major infrastructure initiatives of the past. It begins with background information regarding the definition of infrastructure, historical spending trends, infrastructure needs, and the impact of infrastructure investment. It then provides an overview of major historical infrastructure initiatives, including the nineteenth-century construction of canals and railroads, New Deal capital programs during the Great Depression, and development of the interstate highway system in the 1950s and

1960s. The chapter concludes with a discussion about future infrastructure needs and financing options, drawing on the experiences with the historical infrastructure programs as well as other sources.

BACKGROUND

Public infrastructure usually refers to publicly owned transportation infrastructure (highways, roads, bridges, mass transit, rail, ports, and airports) and water infrastructure (dams, levees, water supply, and wastewater treatment). The term *public infrastructure* can also include other types of infrastructure, such as solid waste and hazardous waste facilities, and social infrastructure (hospitals, schools, prisons, nursing homes, and other public facilities). A broader definition could incorporate privately owned infrastructure that serves a public purpose, such as energy generation and distribution, freight rail, information technology, and telecommunications. The focus of this chapter is transportation and water infrastructure.

Overview of Infrastructure Investments

In the United States, public spending on transportation and water infrastructure as a percentage of gross domestic product (GDP) has been about 2.4 to 3.0 percent since the mid-1950s (see figure 1). The highest percentage

Figure 1. Public spending on transportation and water infrastructure as a percentage of gross domestic product

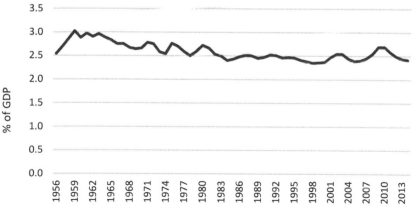

Source: Congressional Budget Office, *Public Spending on Transportation and Water Infrastructure, 1956 to 2014.*

occurred in the late 1950s during the initial stages of the construction of the interstate highway system.

In 2014 public spending on transportation and water infrastructure was about $416 billion. The largest category of spending was highways (40 percent), followed by water utilities (26 percent), which includes water and wastewater treatment facilities (see figure 2). Other major categories include mass transit, aviation, and water resources.

State and local government spending accounts for about three-fourths (77 percent) of the total public spending on transportation and water infrastructure, with the federal government accounting for the remainder (see figure 3). Starting in the 1980s, state and local government spending on infrastructure in real dollars increased significantly, while federal infrastructure remained relatively stable. More recently, from 2003 through 2014, state and local government spending on water and transportation infrastructure decreased by 5 percent and federal government spending declined by 19 percent.[2]

More than half (56 percent) of public spending on water and transportation infrastructure in 2014 was for operations and maintenance, with the remainder being attributable to new or expanded capital (see figure 4). State and local

Figure 2. Public spending on transportation and water infrastructure, 2014

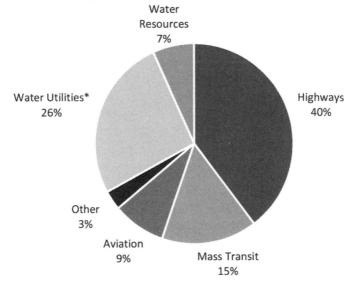

Source: Congressional Budget Office, *Public Spending on Transportation and Water Infrastructure, 1956 to 2014.*
*Includes water and wastewater treatment facilities.

Figure 3. Public spending on transportation and water infrastructure, by level of government, 2014 (in billions of dollars)

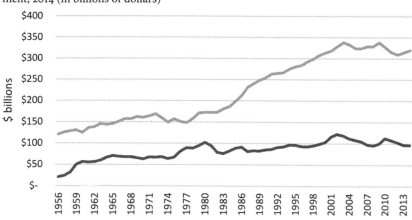

Source: Congressional Budget Office, *Public Spending on Transportation and Water Infrastructure, 1956 to 2014.*

Figure 4. Public infrastructure spending on transportation and water infrastructure by type and level of government, 2014 (in billions of dollars)

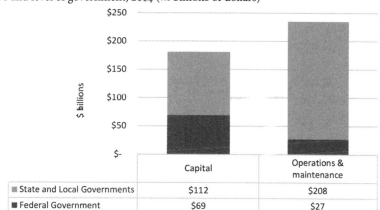

Source: Congressional Budget Office, *Public Spending on Transportation and Water Infrastructure, 1956 to 2014.*

government spending accounted for 62 percent of the total public spending on new water and transportation capital and 89 percent of the total public spending on operations and maintenance. The majority of federal spending (72 percent) is for new or expanded capital, while state and local governments spend more of their funds on operations and maintenance (65 percent).

Infrastructure Condition and Needs

Every four years since 1988, the American Society of Civil Engineers has assigned a grade to infrastructure in the United States. The ASCE uses criteria that address the capacity, condition, funding, future need, operation and maintenance, public safety, resilience, and innovation. In each of the historical report cards, the nation has received a grade of D or D+. The ASCE *2017 Infrastructure Report Card* assigned an overall grade of D+, with some variations among the different types of infrastructure. Among the better grades were rail (B), bridges (C+), ports (C+), and solid waste (C+). The other categories received a D or D+.[3] The ASCE estimates that the United States would need to invest $4.59 trillion over a ten-year period to meet the nation's infrastructure needs.[4]

In 2013 the McKinsey Global Institute issued a report calling for the United States to increase its annual infrastructure investment by 1 percentage point of GDP to eliminate the country's competitive disadvantage. This equates to an increase in public infrastructure investment of about $150 to $180 billion annually. The report referred to a backlog in maintenance and upgrades for U.S. roads, highways, bridges, transit, and water systems.[5]

A third report focuses on the condition of U.S. infrastructure relative to infrastructure in other countries. The World Economic Forum ranked the United States eleventh in the world in 2016–17 for overall quality of infrastructure.[6] This rating is part of a 2016–17 global competitiveness index, in which the United States ranked third in the world. For the infrastructure rating, half of the score is based on the quality of transportation infrastructure and the other half on electricity and telephony infrastructure.

The Impact of Infrastructure Investment

In an analysis prepared for the ASCE, the Economic Development Research Group estimates that each household in America will experience an annual decline of $3,400 in disposable income during the period 2016 to 2025 due to infrastructure deficiencies. This will occur as a result of higher prices due to congested and inefficient transportation systems, delays in personal travel and commuting, and other factors.[7]

The McKinsey Global Institute estimates that increasing the U.S. investment in public infrastructure by 1 percentage point of GDP could result in a 1.4 to 1.7 percent increase in the GDP between 2013 and 2020 and would create 1.5 to 1.8 million jobs for the duration of the investment. The McKinsey Global Institute also estimates that the United States could increase its annual GDP by $600 billion by 2030 if the country took a more efficient approach to project selection. This would help relieve congestion, improve competitiveness, and decrease logistics and supply-chain costs.[8]

The World Economic Forum discusses the importance of transportation infrastructure in getting goods and services to market in an efficient manner and allowing the movement of workers to the most suitable jobs. It also notes the importance of having reliable electricity supplies and an extensive telecommunications network to facilitate the free flow of information.

Over the years, there has been an ongoing debate among scholars about the impact of public infrastructure on the U.S. economy. In the late 1980s, seminal work by David Allan Aschauer found that the elasticity of output with respect to public capital was about 0.34–0.39. Aschauer's findings sparked additional research and debate on the relationship between public infrastructure investments and the economy. In a review of studies conducted over the past twenty years, Alfredo Pereira and Jorge Andraz concluded that the impact of public capital investments on output is positive and significant but much smaller than earlier estimated and that the impact can vary by industry.[9] Pereira and Andraz also recommend that scholars take into account how the infrastructure is financed, since tax increases can counter the positive impact of infrastructure investments on output.

Studies have also found that the impact of infrastructure on the economy can vary depending on the type of infrastructure.[10] Pereira and Andraz found that the largest impact on private investments came from electric and gas facilities, mass transit, and airfields and that highways and streets had a much smaller impact.[11]

With this background information on the importance of public infrastructure, the focus will now shift to a discussion of the historical roots of the nation's infrastructure.

HISTORICAL INFRASTRUCTURE DEVELOPMENT

At various times in the nation's history, the public sector has invested large amounts of funds into the development of new capital infrastructure.

Canals and Railroads

America's early leaders recognized the importance that transportation infrastructure could play in the development of the new nation. James Madison, in the *Federalist Paper No. 14*, referred to the importance of roads and canals in connecting the states.[12] George Washington served as the president of a company that built networks of roads, canals, and locks to expedite transportation between the East and the West.[13]

The most active construction of canals started around 1825 and peaked in 1840.[14] During the period 1815 through 1860, more than four thousand miles of canals were built at an estimated cost of $195 million. Public investment accounted for about 62 percent of the total investment.[15]

State governments, such as New York, Pennsylvania, and Ohio, played an important role in the construction of canals. One of the most historically significant canals was the Erie Canal, which was built by the State of New York and opened in 1825. The Erie Canal revolutionized trade and transportation by creating a waterway connection between Albany, New York, on the Hudson River, and Buffalo, New York, on Lake Erie. This helped facilitate settlement in the western part of the nation and allowed for the shipment of goods at much lower costs. It also helped create an "information superhighway" for the sharing of new ideas, such as abolitionism, women's rights, and various other movements.[16]

This time period also saw the beginning of the use of municipal bonds as a way to finance capital. The first recorded municipal bond was issued by New York State in 1812 to finance a canal. The municipal bond market (which includes bonds issued by state and local governments) grew to $200 million by 1840 and to $1 billion by 1880.[17] As a result of fiscal strain during the recession in 1837, some states defaulted on their bonds. This led some state governments to establish legal debt limits to mitigate future problems.[18]

The federal government's role in canals was more limited. In 1807 the U.S. Senate passed a resolution that directed the U.S. Treasury Department to prepare a report on how the federal government should address transportation problems. The secretary of the treasurer, Albert Gallatin, submitted a report on roads and canals that proposed a comprehensive plan for a system of canals and turnpikes to be funded by the federal government.[19] This plan met resistance from government leaders, some of whom questioned whether the federal government had the constitutional authority to build canals and roads. The plan was not formally adopted; however, following the War of 1812, many of the proposed projects were eventually completed using a combination of state, local, and private funding.[20] In the 1820s, the federal government provided funding for several major canals.

By the 1850s, the construction of canals had declined and more emphasis was being placed on railroads. Private companies developed and owned most of the railroads, while the state governments issued charters and owned much of the rights-of-way. The private companies financed construction through loans and stock and, at times, entered into barter arrangements in which stock was exchanged for labor.

State governments provided financial assistance for rail projects in the form of stock subscriptions, loans, or loan guarantees. State governments in the South contributed the highest amounts, financing more than 55 percent of the total costs of railroad construction in the region before 1861. Nationwide, the public contributions in cash or credit were about 25–30 percent or more of the total rail construction prior to 1861.[21]

The federal government also provided loans to the railroads, with the amounts varying depending on the terrain. In 1862 Congress passed the Pacific Railway Act, which led to construction of the first transcontinental railroad. The Union Pacific built from Council Bluffs, Iowa, heading west, and the Central Pacific Railroad built from Sacramento, California, heading east, and they eventually joined in Promontory, Utah. The federal government provided land grants and long-term loans for this project.[22]

Much of the federal government's contributions to railroads were in the form of land grants.[23] During the period 1861–72, the federal government contributed more than 100 million acres in land grants to railroad companies. The federal land could be used for rights-of-way, and the adjacent land could be developed or sold to generate revenues. The State of Texas also contributed about thirty-two million acres of land, mostly after the Civil War.[24]

As rail became more developed, the public contributions declined. During the period 1861–90, the public contributions were somewhat less than $350 million, with local governments accounting for about $175 million. After 1873 the public contributions amounted to no more than a negligible fraction of the total rail investments.[25]

RELEVANCE TO TODAY'S APPROACH TO INFRASTRUCTURE   The early developments of canals and railroads demonstrated the importance of transportation infrastructure in facilitating commerce and development and in building connections within and among states. The early years also demonstrated the role that private companies can play, along with their limitations. Private companies played the lead role in building and operating railroads but, in the early years, needed governmental assistance. This time period also saw the first use of state and local government bonds, the growth of the bond market, and the eventual creation of legal debt limits to help state and local governments avoid future bond defaults.

New Deal Infrastructure Programs

Another major influx of funds into the development of new capital occurred through the New Deal programs that were initiated by President Franklin Delano Roosevelt in response to the Great Depression. Facing an unemployment rate of close to 25 percent and a dearth of private-sector spending, the federal government invested billions of dollars in putting people to work on infrastructure and other projects. Three of the major New Deal programs had an impact on infrastructure: the Civilian Conservation Corps (CCC, 1933–42), the Public Works Administration (PWA, 1933–42), and the Works Progress Administration (WPA, 1935–43), which in 1939 was renamed the Work Projects Administration.

One of the most popular New Deal programs was the Civilian Conservation Corps program, which hired young unemployed men ages eighteen to twenty-five to work on natural resource conservation projects. The participants, which numbered from about 250,000 to 500,000 at any one time, were stationed at twenty-six hundred camps that were dispersed throughout the states.[26] The men worked on nearby projects and received wages, which they shared with their families. They also received vocational and other types of schooling. Over the life of the program, the CCC program employed about 3 million men.[27]

CCC participants worked on structural improvements (bridges, fire towers, and museums), transportation (roads, trails, and airport landing strips), erosion and flood-control projects, reforestation and wildlife projects, and various other types of projects.[28] The program was supported through the Department of Labor, which selected the participants; the Department of Agriculture and the Department of the Interior, which selected the projects; and the U.S. Army, which set up and managed the camps.[29]

In 1933 the National Industrial Recovery Act established the Public Works Administration. The act authorized $3.3 billion for public works projects, including federal projects (roads and ships), as well as state and local government projects. The PWA also took over projects that had been initiated under a loan program started by the Hoover administration. For new state and local government projects, the PWA program provided federal grants for a portion of the costs and offered loans for the remainder of the costs.

President Roosevelt established the Special Board for Public Works to serve as an advisory board for the PWA program. The board consisted of the secretaries of the Departments of War, Agriculture, Treasury, Commerce, Labor, and Interior; the director of the Bureau of the Budget; and the attorney general. Harold L. Ickes, secretary of the interior, served as the chair of the board and as the PWA administrator.[30]

Ickes was known for ensuring careful scrutiny of the proposed projects. This was a balancing act because the PWA was under pressure to start projects quickly to help stimulate the economy. At that time, many state and local governments lacked experience in designing and administering public works projects and faced legal constraints that limited their ability to take on new debt. The PWA worked with communities to develop new methods of financing, including the use of public authorities and revenue bonds.[31]

The PWA program undertook about thirty-four thousand projects, including many of the largest and most visible of the New Deal projects, such as the Boulder Dam (later renamed Hoover Dam) and the Triborough Bridge in New York City. The PWA funded about $5 billion in grants and loans for the construction of schools, hospitals, libraries, other public buildings, highways, water and sewer systems, electric power systems, and flood-control and reclamation projects.[32] The PWA also built many airport buildings, including a terminal building at Washington National Airport, later renamed Ronald Reagan Washington National Airport.[33]

The federal government imposed controls, including rules related to procurement, labor practices, accounting, and other business procedures. The federal government also assigned a resident engineer-inspector to each site to ensure adherence to federal regulations and to prevent kickbacks. The federal government required at least three audits, and the PWA established an inspection division to follow up on complaints about specific projects. Leighninger notes that these practices were "quite successful in keeping the many attempts to make political or financial profit from becoming full-blown scandals."[34]

A third New Deal program, the Works Progress Administration, was created in 1935 to promote economic development and put people to work. This program was headed by Harry Hopkins, a social worker who was also the secretary of commerce. The WPA provided employment for about eight million people and spent about $4 billion on projects.[35]

Local governments and their various agencies initiated and planned the majority of WPA projects, including the identification of the types of labor that would be needed. The unskilled workers were to come from local relief roles. Initially, there was no local government financial contribution requirements. However, after January 1, 1940, the WPA sponsor contributions in aggregate for a state had to be at least 25 percent, but there was no minimum requirement for individual projects. In practice, local contributions were about 10 percent in mid-1936 and about 30 percent in the final years of WPA.

The original focus was on roads, rural electrification, water conservation, sanitation, and flood control. Legislation passed in 1936 added public buildings, parks, public utilities, airports, and transit facilities. In 1937 the scope was expanded to include nonconstruction educational, professional, and women's projects.[36] By 1941 the WPA's focus was on defense-related projects.

The program had multiple stages of review, including the WPA, the Bureau of the Budget, the Advisory Committee on Allotments, and the president. The Advisory Committee on Allotments, which included government officials and representatives of labor, farming, the American Bankers Association, and the U.S. Conference of Mayors, served as the main decision-making entity and adviser to President Roosevelt.[37]

The final report on the WPA program described the following accomplishments: "Building or improving 651,000 miles of roads, erection or improvement of 125,110 buildings of all kinds, installation of 16,100 miles of water mains and distribution lines, installation of 24,300 miles of sewerage facilities, construction and improvement of many airport facilities, including landing fields, runways, and terminal buildings."[38] The report stated that sponsors of projects contributed $2.8 billion and the federal government $10.1 billion.

In 1939 the administration of the PWA and WPA were combined into a single agency called the Federal Works Agency. The PWA program ended in 1942 and the WPA in 1943.

RELEVANCE TO TODAY'S APPROACH TO INFRASTRUCTURE   The New Deal infrastructure programs embraced Keynesian economic policy by implementing public works spending to stimulate the economy and decrease unemployment. This use of capital spending has continued into modern times, as evidenced by the most recent appropriation of federal stimulus funds during the Great Recession.

The tying of a jobs program to the construction of capital projects helped restore people's dignity,[39] but it also impacted the types of projects that were undertaken. Plus, the New Deal programs were viewed as temporary, which may have made it difficult to undertake multiyear planning.

The New Deal programs created a vast array of infrastructure that has had a lasting impact on society. The programs resulted in projects that served a functional purpose but also included projects with aesthetic, cultural, or historical value. Thus, infrastructure was viewed in a broader context in terms of meeting multiple aspects of societal needs.

The New Deal's decentralized approach in which the federal government provided funding and state and local governments identified projects and oversaw the construction of the projects has become a regular practice in the United States. At the federal level, the New Deal program demonstrated the need for and ability of federal agencies to work together toward a common national goal.

Early Roads and the Development of the Interstate Highway System

The next major federal infrastructure program was the development of the interstate highway system in the 1950s and 1960s.

In the early years, local governments built roads within their jurisdictions. Lacking sufficient revenues, the governments often required men in the community to contribute labor to construct and maintain the roads.[40] Private firms also built roads, but they focused on roads that connected communities and provided access to agricultural products in rural areas.[41] These roads, which were called turnpikes, charged tolls; however, over time, the revenues were often insufficient to repay investors and maintain the roads. This resulted in maintenance deferrals, which made the roads less attractive to haulers.[42] By the 1860s, many of these turnpikes were not fiscally sustainable and were turned over to local governments.[43]

The federal government also played a role in the development of early roads. In the early 1800s, Congress proposed using funds from land sales in Ohio to build a road from Cumberland, Maryland, to Wheeling, Virginia (now part of West Virginia). President Thomas Jefferson authorized the road in 1806, construction started in 1811, and the road to Wheeling was completed in 1819.[44] The Cumberland Road (later renamed the National Pike) was the first major road built by the federal government.[45] The Army Corps of Engineers continued construction of the road west of Wheeling.

The federal government considered converting the road into a toll road to generate funds for the maintenance of the road. However, critics raised questions about the constitutionality of that proposal, and in 1822 President James Monroe vetoed the legislation. The federal government then transferred ownership of the road to the respective state governments. The Army Corps of Engineers installed toll gates, and the states operated the roads as toll roads.

Over time, the U.S. Supreme Court provided increased clarity regarding the federal government's authority in regard to roads. In 1824 the U.S. Supreme Court in *Gibbons v. Ogden* ruled that Congress had the power to regulate interstate commerce under the Commerce Clause of the U.S. Constitution.

Later, in 1907, the U.S. Supreme Court ruled in *Wilson v. Shaw* that the Commerce Clause allows Congress the power to construct interstate highways and canals.[46]

In 1913 a private entrepreneur developed the Lincoln Highway, which was one of the first transcontinental auto routes in the United States. It connected existing roads spanning from New York to California, covering thirteen states at the time (another state was later added). Other similar initiatives followed.[47]

Over time, various federal actions laid the foundation for the interstate highway program. In 1916 Congress authorized federal matching grants over five years for highway construction and in 1921 reauthorized the grant program for an additional five years. In 1922 the military prepared the Pershing Map, which identified roads that would be needed for defense purposes in time of war. And in 1926 a Joint Board on Interstate Highways, which included three people from the federal Bureau of Public Roads and twenty-one state highway officials, created a highway numbering system that used odd numbers for north–south roads and even numbers for east–west roads.[48]

Federal legislation passed in 1938 directed the Bureau of Public Roads to conduct a study on the feasibility of a toll-financed highway system that would include several east–west and north–south superhighways. The bureau concluded that a toll-financed system would not generate sufficient funds to be self-supporting and instead recommended a 26,700-mile network of interregional highways.[49]

Six years later, federal legislation called for the designation of up to 40,000 miles to connect metropolitan areas and serve the national defense. States submitted requests for highways to be included, and the Department of Defense reviewed those proposals. On August 2, 1947, the federal works administrator and the commissioner of public roads announced the designation of the first 37,700 miles, including about 2,900 miles of urban thoroughfares. In 1955 the U.S. Bureau of Public Roads released a document referred to as the "Yellow Book" that included maps showing the general routing of urban interstates.[50]

President Dwight Eisenhower led the effort to generate funding for the interstate highway system. He had previously participated in the 1919 Motor Transport Corps Convoy, which experienced many problems while traveling from Washington, D.C., to California to test the nation's highway system's readiness for war. Plus, Eisenhower had studied and been impressed with Germany's network of rural superhighways.[51] President Eisenhower stated,

"The country urgently needs a modernized interstate highway system to relieve existing congestion, to provide for the expected growth of motor vehicle traffic, to strengthen the Nation's defenses, to reduce the toll of human life exacted each year in highway accidents, and to promote economic development."[52]

The Federal-Aid Highway Act of 1956 and the Highway Revenue Act of 1956 (combined into Public Law 84-627) authorized the construction of and funding for the interstate highway system. The system, which was named the National System of Interstate and Defense Highways, included 41,000 miles. Congress approved a 90–10 percent split between federal and state and local funding and authorized $25 billion for interstate highway projects for the fiscal years 1957 through 1969.

The plan was to connect the nation's 209 cities that had a population of greater than 50,000. The system would primarily be divided highways, with only about 7,000 miles of two-lane roads. The plan incorporated some existing toll roads. Funding was to occur through the Highway Trust Fund, which would obtain revenues from numerous road-user taxes, including an increase in the federal fuel tax from 2 to 3 cents per gallon, and new excise taxes on motor vehicle purchases, oil, replacement tires, and other replacement parts. (In 1970 most of the revenue sources other than the motor-fuel tax were eliminated.)[53] The funding was initially apportioned based on the formula used for the federal-aid primary category, which was based on mileage, area, and population. Later funds were allocated on the basis of the ratio of the costs of completing the system within a state relative to the cost of completion for the system as a whole.[54]

The development of the interstate highway program occurred over the following decade, with additional funds bringing the total investment to about $129 billion, which included $114 billion in federal funds, for the construction of about 42,000 miles.[55] States built the roads to conform to design standards that had been agreed to by the Bureau of Public Roads and an association of state highway officials.

The interstate program encountered various challenges along the way. Funding shortfalls led to an increase in the gas tax to 4 cents a gallon. Plus, there were problems associated with right-of-way acquisition and land-speculation schemes.

Critics claimed that the new interstates were displacing city residents, particularly those with low incomes, and that the interstates were creating "walls" that divided cities. Author and social scientist Lewis Mumford stated that the interstate program was bound to lead to destruction, given that it had been founded on "a very insufficient study" of highways rather than transportation and relied on "blunders of one-dimensional thinking."[56] Opposition from local residents in some urban areas led to changes in the planned interstate routes.

Daniel Moynihan, a professor and later a U.S. senator, expressed concerns about the need to do highway planning in a broader metropolitan land-use planning context that considered economic and social objectives. He also advocated for funding flexibility so cities could choose to use the funds for mass transit instead of highways.[57]

Overall, the interstate highway system made significant advancements in decreasing the amount of time it takes to travel cross-country and in reducing highway fatality rates.[58] Today the interstate highway system consists of 47,814 miles and accounts for about 25 percent of the total vehicle miles traveled in the United States.[59] According to the Federal Highway Administration, the interstate highway system is the safest road system in the country.[60]

RELEVANCE TO TODAY'S APPROACH TO INFRASTRUCTURE   The development of the nation's interstate highway system has been referred to as one of the "wonders of the modern world."[61] This undertaking demonstrated the significant results that can occur when the federal government works collaboratively with state governments. The approach used to design and implement the interstate highway system involved a strong federal role, combined with a significant role for state governments regarding the routes, design standards, and project construction. Opposition from residents in some urban areas serves as a reminder of the importance of consulting with local government officials and other community leaders on projects that will have substantial local impacts.

The construction of the interstate highway system demonstrated the value of having designated revenue sources, in particular the federal motor-fuel tax, along with the willingness to increase revenues if necessary. But the undertaking fell short in terms of including a provision to finance the future maintenance of the roads. This signifies the importance of addressing life-cycle costs, which include not only the acquisition or construction costs of infrastructure but also the operation and maintenance costs throughout the life of the asset and, if applicable, disposal costs.

Having discussed the historical undertaking of much of the nation's infrastructure, the focus now shifts to looking to infrastructure needs and financing for the future.

INFRASTRUCTURE NEEDS AND FINANCING IN THE FUTURE

As the Trump administration moves forward with its infrastructure plan, the need to identify capital priorities and funding sources will become increasingly important.

Strengthening Transportation Systems

Throughout the nation's history, the development of transportation infrastructure has had major impacts on commerce and the daily lives of people. Transportation infrastructure provides firms with access to labor and product markets and allows individuals access to employment, education, goods and services, and recreation. As noted with the early development of canals, transportation infrastructure can also support the sharing of new ideas.

The provision of transportation infrastructure in the United States continues to be decentralized and complex. The majority of roads are owned by state (19 percent) and local governments (77 percent), and most of the freight rail is operated by private companies.[62] To sustain and grow the economy, the different transportation modes located throughout the country need to be integrated into an effective transportation system.

In developing a national infrastructure plan, what insights can be gleaned from past massive capital undertakings, such as the ones described in this chapter? First, the federal government needs to treat state and local governments as important partners in the development and implementation of improvements to the transportation system. Throughout history state and local governments have identified, constructed, owned, and maintained much of the nation's transportation infrastructure. They are the governments closest to the people, and their views and perspectives need to be taken into account.

Past infrastructure projects, in particular the interstate highway system, demonstrate the important role the federal government can play in facilitating projects that span multiple states. In current times, that could include projects such as high-speed rail or enhancements to the air-traffic control system. It could also include federal financing for a portion of large transportation infrastructure projects in urban areas that directly impact more than one state or have significant spillover impacts on other states.

Past infrastructure initiatives also demonstrate the value of identifying national interests or goals that can be pursued through infrastructure programs. For example, during the New Deal, the infrastructure programs were designed to stimulate the economy and provide jobs, which influenced the types of projects that were undertaken. During the development of the interstate highway system, President Eisenhower noted the need to relieve congestion, facilitate expected traffic growth, strengthen defense, and improve highway safety. This resulted in a system of connected roads with limited access points and a standardized design to promote safety.

The federal government might choose to focus on a goal such as growing the national economy or improving environmental sustainability. To facilitate economic growth, the federal government could fund projects that address bottlenecks in key components of the national transportation system. To address environmental sustainability, the federal government could fund projects such as mass transit or provide incentives to encourage telecommuting or congestion-based pricing on toll roads.

In developing a national infrastructure plan, consideration also needs to be given to technology advancements. In the early years, canals revolutionized travel but later became obsolete with the development of faster and more efficient modes of transportation. Policy makers need to consider emerging technologies as well as prospective technologies that may occur in the future.

Currently, one of the most highly publicized technological advancements is the advent of the driverless vehicle. State and local governments are addressing the types of infrastructure-related investments that will be needed to support this development, such as sensors that communicate with moving vehicles and improved pavement marking and road signs.[63] The National Conference of State Legislatures reports that as of September 2017, thirty-three states had introduced related legislation in 2017 and twenty states had passed related legislation.[64] Congress has also been addressing policy issues related to autonomous vehicles.

Other technological advancements also merit consideration. For example, technological advancements in construction materials and techniques may prolong the useful life of roads and bridges, and interactive signage with updates on weather conditions and congestion may improve safety.[65] Cell phone applications continue to develop, such as applications that can reroute drivers to avoid congested areas. Advances are also occurring in toll-road technology, such as methods for applying differential pricing depending on the time of the day or congestion.

In looking to the future, social and demographic trends are also relevant. Compared to the past, young people drive less now and make greater use of public transit, bicycles, and ride-hailing services.[66] Planning for transportation and related infrastructure will need to acknowledge these evolving trends. On the other end of the age spectrum, seniors who no longer drive require transportation options. This is especially a concern in rural areas.[67]

In summary, the federal government will need to work collaboratively with representatives from state and local governments to develop transportation systems that will achieve national goals and prepare the nation for the future. It will be important to develop a strategic vision for the future and identify what type of transportation infrastructure will be needed to support that vision.

Prioritizing Infrastructure Maintenance

Historically, the federal government has invested primarily in new infrastructure rather than the maintenance of existing infrastructure. The latter has primarily been the responsibility of state and local governments. However, given the magnitude of the infrastructure maintenance needs, this policy needs to be reevaluated.

Much of the interstate highway system that was built in the 1950s and 1960s is in need of major repair or replacement. Although states are replacing portions of the interstate highway system, a major overhaul of the network would be a vast undertaking—one in which the federal government likely would need to play the lead role, especially in terms of funding. The estimated net economic benefits of recapitalizing the entire interstate highway system is over $1.6 trillion.[68]

In the mid-1990s, Howard Rosen expressed a similar concern regarding the infrastructure that was developed during the New Deal. He stated, "If there is a 'New Frontier' in public works, it may involve the best possible maintenance of New Deal and other public works investments that have formed the nation's infrastructure. Providing state and local governments with maintenance technologies may be a legitimate and significant federal role that continues the Rooseveltian tradition in public works."[69]

The American Society of Civil Engineers provides estimates of the nation's maintenance needs and the impact of insufficient maintenance. The most recent estimates indicate that about two-thirds of the nation's $836 billion in highway infrastructure needs are related to maintenance. About 20 percent of the nation's highways had poor pavement in 2014, with urban roads being worse than rural roads (32 percent compared to 14 percent). The lack of sufficient maintenance resulted in $112 billion in additional vehicle repair costs in 2014. Transit infrastructure has about a $90 billion maintenance backlog. In the water sector, there are about 240,000 water-main breaks annually. Leaky pipes result in a loss of about 14 to 18 percent of the daily treated water.[70]

From an economics perspective, governments should invest in public infrastructure projects that yield the highest net present value. Funds invested in maintaining and repairing infrastructure may have higher returns than funds spent on new infrastructure, since the large initial capital construction outlays have already occurred. The Congressional Budget Office concluded that federal highway spending could yield greater overall net benefits by increasing spending on major repairs by 1 percent and decreasing spending on expansion by 2 percent.[71]

The federal government could consider different types of funding, depending on the nature of the capital project. Michael Pagano, an urban scholar, recommends federal matching grants for the repair and maintenance of existing infrastructure and federal loans for new and expanded infrastructure.[72] He also recommends the use of pricing policies and other financial practices that take into account not only the acquisition or construction costs but also the maintenance and operation costs over the life of the asset.

Ensuring Health and Safety

Over the years, the federal government has invested in infrastructure projects to improve health and safety. For example, one of the driving forces for the creation of the interstate highway system was to improve traveler safety.[73] Plus, currently the federal government provides capitalization funds for state revolving-fund (SRF) programs that provide loans for the financing of local water and wastewater projects.

However, major events have drawn public attention to the need for further infrastructure improvements to protect public health and safety. This includes events such as the levy break in New Orleans during Hurricane Katrina, the I-35 West bridge collapse in Minnesota that killed 13 people and injured 145 people, major flooding in coastal areas and other parts of the country, destruction from natural disasters and fires, and the lead in the water pipes in Flint, Michigan.

Local governments can take the lead on many health and safety and environmental infrastructure projects, but they need financial, technical, policy, and legal support from the federal and state governments. Past infrastructure initiatives demonstrate the benefits from having support and collaboration at all levels of government.

Local water and wastewater projects play a critical role in ensuring public health. However, federal funding for the SRF programs that finance water and wastewater projects has been flat or declining since fiscal year (FY) 2010.[74] Congress initially viewed the federal funding as a temporary source to capitalize the SRF programs, but state officials note that the programs are not sustainable without continued federal funding or changes to the programs.[75] Recent congressional proposals have called for options such as increasing federal funding for SRF programs, establishing a federal water infrastructure trust fund that has a dedicated revenue source, or creating a permanent Water Infrastructure Finance and Innovations Act program to provide long-term, low-cost supplemental loans for regionally and nationally significant water projects.[76] (Federal legislation authorized a five-year WIFIA pilot program in 2014.)

The nation also needs resilient infrastructure that can help mitigate the losses from downpours and natural disasters, which have become more severe and frequent.[77] During Hurricane Sandy in 2012, New York and New Jersey experienced storm surges that caused millions of gallons of untreated sewage to spill into waterways.[78] The more recent devastation from Hurricane Harvey and Hurricane Maria emphasizes the importance of infrastructure that can facilitate drainage and maintain access to or ensure timely restoration of critical services such as water, electricity, and transportation.[79]

Some local governments are pursuing infrastructure strategies such as creating seawalls, constructing or expanding tunnels to absorb water, establishing new building codes that require more resilient homes and business structures, and imposing storm-water fees to generate funds to pay for related infrastructure. Some cities are also developing green infrastructure such as rooftop vegetation, porous pavements, and expansion of wetlands.

Local governments are also undertaking infrastructure initiatives to help ensure that future generations will have access to drinkable water, clean air, and energy. For example, some wastewater utilities are reusing wastewater to decrease the demand for freshwater or generating energy from digestive methane to operate their facilities. Some public energy utilities are installing infrastructure or creating policies to increase their use of renewable energy, such as solar and wind energy, and are implementing programs to promote energy conservation. Some urban areas are investing in mass transit, which can result in less pollution and more efficient use of resources.

In summary, investments in water and wastewater systems, resilient infrastructure, and infrastructure initiatives that promote the conservation of natural resources help provide public health and safety for current residents and promote environmental sustainability for future generations. But local governments cannot do all of this on their own. They need support and assistance from the federal and state governments.

Financing Infrastructure

Identifying priority infrastructure investments is critical, but the public sector also has to identify ways to fund those investments. Various types of federal, state, and local government funding sources, as well as private-sector funds, have been used in the past to support infrastructure.

HIGHWAYS   During the development of the interstate highway system, the motor-fuel tax emerged as the main revenue source for the funding of highways. When the interstate highway system legislation was passed, Congress approved an increase in the motor-fuel tax rate to generate additional funding. When there was a financial shortfall during the construction of the interstate highway system, Congress increased the rate again.

However, during the past twenty years, Congress has been reluctant to increase the motor-fuel tax rate. It currently remains at the same level as it was in 1993, 18.4 cents per gallon on gasoline and 24.4 cents per gallon on diesel.[80] This, combined with a decrease in fuel consumption due to more energy-efficient vehicles and changes in driving habits, has resulted in financial shortfalls in the Highway Trust Fund.

The Congressional Research Service (CRS) estimates that during the period FY 2012 through FY 2025, the revenues generated for the Highway Trust Fund, on average, will be about $20 billion less per year than the amount needed to finance the current federal surface transportation program.[81] Since 2008 Congress has transferred $140 billion from the General Fund to the Highway Trust Fund, including $70 billion that was authorized in the passage of the Fixing America's Surface Transportation (FAST) Act in 2015.[82]

Proposals have been made to increase the federal motor-fuel tax rate and to index it to inflation. The administrative costs associated with this option would be relatively low since the collection process is already in place. A higher tax rate would generate additional revenues and could be used to capture external costs from driving, such as the costs of pollution, climate change, and dependence on foreign oil. This would help increase economic efficiency by having users pay based on the marginal costs their usage of roads imposes on society.[83]

However, a more economically efficient approach might be to base a tax on the number of vehicle miles driven.[84] Compared to the motor-fuel tax, a mileage tax could be more directly tied to the cost of pavement repair and be less impacted by energy-efficient vehicles. The mileage tax rate could be fixed or could vary based on factors such as the time of day or how much pollution a vehicle emits. This tax would forge a more direct relationship between those who pay the tax and those who benefit the most from roads and could be used to mitigate pollution and congestion.

A Congressional Research Service report identified the following potential concerns with a mileage tax relative to the motor-fuel tax: public concerns about privacy;[85] higher costs to establish, collect, and enforce; the administrative challenges of billing about 256 million vehicles (compared to 850 taxpayers for the motor-fuel tax, since it is collected when the fuel leaves the refinery or tank farm); and the potential for opposition to rate increases (similar to that facing the motor-fuel tax).[86] If there is an emerging trend for people to drive less, a tax based on vehicle miles may face future challenges.

Toll roads represent another revenue option. Toll roads are a growing source of revenue in more than thirty states.[87] Currently, about fifty-nine hundred miles of toll roads in the United States generate about $13 billion in revenues annually.[88] Toll-road technology has improved so that now sensors can be used to assess charges rather than having vehicles stop at a toll booth. Toll roads can also use congestion pricing as a means to encourage people to drive during nonrush hours, thus decreasing the overall capacity demand on roads.

However, there are also concerns regarding increased reliance on toll roads. The Congressional Research Service concluded, "Whatever policies Congress adopt, tolls are likely to play only a limited role in funding surface transportation projects."[89] The CRS notes that the costs of toll collection often exceed 10 percent of revenue, even when tolls are collected electronically. This is much higher than the costs of collecting the federal motor-fuel tax, which is estimated at about 1 percent of revenues. The CRS also cautions that many roads do not have enough traffic to generate sufficient toll revenue to cover construction, maintenance, and collection costs and that elected officials may be reluctant to raise toll rates.

DEBT FINANCING   Governments need revenue sources to support infrastructure projects, but they can also benefit from the ability to obtain debt financing at low interest rates. Dating back to the 1800s, and continuing into modern times, state and local government bonds have played an important role in financing infrastructure. Federal loans have also been and will continue to be instrumental in financing infrastructure.

The tax-exempt status of municipal bonds is very important in the financing of public infrastructure. More than fifty thousand individual units of governments have outstanding municipal bonds, which collectively total about $3.6 trillion in par value. According to the National League of Cities, more than three-fourths of public infrastructure is funded with tax-exempt municipal bonds, which results in savings of about 20–25 percent in interest costs.[90] State and local governments and their professional associations have lobbied hard to maintain the tax-exempt status of municipal bonds and will continue to do so as the federal government engages in tax-reform discussions.

Some officials have called for the reinstatement of taxable bonds that are subsidized by a direct subsidy payment from the federal government to state and local governments that issue the bonds. In response to the Great

Recession, Congress authorized state and local governments to issue tax-able bonds called Build America Bonds, in which the federal government paid a 35 percent interest subsidy to the issuer. The U.S. Treasury Department estimated that state and local governments issued 2,275 separate BAB issues, which financed more than $181 billion in infrastructure projects.[91] The BAB program expired at the end of 2010.

Taxable bonds with a federal subsidy provision offer a number of advantages. They can attract investors, such as pension funds, that do not benefit from the tax-exempt status of traditional municipal bonds. These types of bonds can be a more cost-effective type of subsidy than tax-exempt bonds, in which a portion of the federal subsidy results in savings to individuals with high incomes.[92] This type of bond program could also increase transparency, since it would be subject to the annual federal appropriations process. However, being part of the annual appropriations process could result in more uncertainty and the possibility of a decrease in the federal role compared to the long, stable history of tax-exempt bonds.[93]

The federal government currently administers several programs, such as the state revolving-fund programs, WIFIA, the Transportation Infrastructure Finance and Innovation Act (TIFIA) program, and the Railroad Rehabilitation and Improvement Financing program, that offer loans or loan guarantees for certain types of infrastructure projects. These programs allow state and local governments, and, in some cases, private firms, to obtain low-cost financing. Some projects may also qualify for tax-exempt private-activity bonds (PABs).

Another option for providing low-cost financing would be to create a national infrastructure bank. The bank could operate as an independent government-owned corporation and use public seed funds, along with private capital, to make loans or loan guarantees for infrastructure projects. Advocates note this type of bank could decrease project costs, increase investment opportunities, decrease the impact of politics on project section, increase incentives for private-sector participation, and help facilitate regional and interjurisdictional projects.[94] The bank could also require borrowers to fund maintenance reserve funds and to conduct periodic asset-integrity inspections.[95]

Expanding the Role of the Private Sector

President Trump's infrastructure plans call for an expansion of the role of the private sector. This is in recognition that the private sector can play a role in the financing of infrastructure and can also offer other benefits.

Historically, the private sector has played an important role in the development of public infrastructure. Some of the earliest toll roads were built and operated by private firms. Most of the early railroad construction was undertaken by private firms with financial assistance from the federal and state governments. Today, private companies own and operate the majority of infrastructure related to freight rail, telecommunications, and energy. These are areas that generally have sufficient demand, profits, and stability to attract private investors and operators.

In discussing the role of the private sector, it is important to distinguish between "financing" and "funding." Financing refers to the means used to generate sufficient up-front cash to pay for an infrastructure project, while funding refers to the revenues than can be used to pay for the costs. Private firms may be willing to provide financing for public infrastructure, but there need to be sufficient revenues, generated from either the infrastructure or some other source, to provide a return on private investments.

One option is to expand the use of public-private partnerships (P3s). Although there is no standard definition of a P3, the World Bank uses the following definition: "a long-term contract between a private party and a government entity, for providing a public asset or service, in which the private party bears significant risk and management responsibility and remuneration is linked to performance."[96]

P3s may be feasible for infrastructure projects that generate a revenue stream, such as water utilities, toll roads, and airports, but questions arise regarding how well P3s can work for non-revenue-generating infrastructure and for smaller projects, which make up the bulk of state and local capital spending.[97] One possibility is to support P3s through revenue sources other than user charges related to a specific asset. A July 2017 New York Times op-ed piece by former secretary of transportation Mary Peters and coauthor Samar Barend noted that only eight of the eighteen public-private transportation projects undertaken since 2010 transferred toll or revenue risk to the private sector. The other projects paid the private firms an availability payment for the use of the asset based on its condition and accessibility.[98]

Peters and Barend identified successful public-private partnerships such as central terminal renovations at La Guardia Airport, expansion of Denver's mass transit system, and construction of the Port Miami Tunnel. They also noted that public-private partnerships can help rural areas, as demonstrated by a $1 billion project to expand a California university that mainly serves rural students and a $2 billion project in North Dakota to alleviate flooding.[99]

P3s offer a number of potential advantages. They can lead to cost savings by shifting the risk of cost increases, delays, and revenue performance to private investors.[100] P3s can also include contract provisions that address the maintenance of the infrastructure. The use of a design-build approach, a type of P3 in which the same firm designs and constructs the road or facility, when used appropriately can decrease the time to complete a project, reduce the costs, and encourage more innovation in design and construction.[101]

However, care must be taken to preserve the public interest when undertaking P3s.[102] This is an area in which the federal and state governments could, through the establishment of dedicated units, assist in the development and negotiation of P3 agreements. This is already occurring to an extent through entities such as the Federal Highway Administration Center for Innovative Finance Support, which conducts research and training and provides technical assistance related to P3s and other revenue options, such as PABs and TIFIA.[103] Several states (California, Michigan, and Virginia) have also been leaders in regards to establishing a dedicated unit to address P3s.[104]

Another means for expanding the private sector's role in infrastructure development is to offer tax incentives for public infrastructure investments. One proposal, which was advanced during the 2016 presidential election, calls for $137 billion in federal tax credits for companies that finance transportation projects. Tax incentives have been used in low-income housing development and more recently for renewable-energy projects. Critics of tax credits for infrastructure projects caution that tax credits may encourage private firms to pursue the most profitable infrastructure, which may not necessarily be the most needed infrastructure. They also note that the tax credits may end up being used for infrastructure projects that would have been undertaken in the absence of tax credits.[105]

In summary, private firms have played an important role in the construction and provision of public infrastructure throughout the history of the nation. The role of private firms has evolved over time. Today, P3s can be viewed as an opportunity for incorporating the expertise of private firms, sharing risks, and attracting private financing. But these firms expect to be compensated for their role. So, the key to an effective P3, as well as an effective tax-credit program, is to seek a balance between the needs of the private firms and the public-sector goals for the project or program.

CONCLUSION

Public infrastructure plays a critical role in the nation's economy as well as the daily lives of individuals. The nation's approach to the provision of infrastructure is a complex array of different types of providers, including federal, state, and local governments as well as private companies, in addition to different financing mechanisms. As illustrated by the development of the interstate highway system and the New Deal capital projects, a significant amount of planning, collaboration, and public support is needed for the undertaking of infrastructure improvements.

As the nation seeks to develop an infrastructure plan for the future, it will be important to recognize the importance of existing infrastructure. The government has invested huge amounts of funds in existing highways, water systems, and other public facilities. These infrastructure and structures need to be maintained. Although it is politically appealing to invest in new infrastructure and to discuss new technology such as driverless vehicles, there remains a critical need to invest in the maintenance of existing infrastructure.

One of the biggest challenges will be rallying support for sufficient funding of infrastructure maintenance and improvements. When infrastructure is functioning well, people may take it for granted. They may not know that infrastructure maintenance has been deferred. Therefore, it is incumbent on government leaders to undertake efforts to better educate the public on the importance and costs of infrastructure investments and the need to finance these investments.

Drawing on the expertise and resources of the private sector can be advantageous, but private firms are motivated by profits and will seek a return on their investments. Although the private sector can play an important role in the future investment in infrastructure, it is not going to solve the funding challenges.

Ultimately, the public needs to understand that providing funding for public infrastructure, including the maintenance of that infrastructure, is an investment in the future. This investment will help support and grow the economy and have a positive impact on the daily lives of people.

Notes

1. *President Trump's Plan to Rebuild America's Infrastructure*, White House blog, June 8, 2017, https://www.whitehouse.gov/blog/2017/06/08/president-trumps-plan-rebuild-americas-infrastructure.

2. Congressional Budget Office, *Public Spending on Transportation and Water Infrastructure, 1956 to 2014*, March 2015, www.cbo.gov/publication/49910.

3. The other ASCE categories include aviation, dams, drinking water, energy, hazardous waste, inland waterways, levees, public parks and recreation, roads, schools, transit, and wastewater.

4. American Society of Civil Engineers, "2017 Infrastructure Report Card," https://www.infrastructurereportcard.org/making-the-grade/report-card-history/.

5. Susan Lund et al., "Game Changers: Five Opportunities for US Growth and Renewal," McKinsey Global Institute, 2013, http://www.mckinsey.com/global-themes/americas/us-game-changers, 88.

6. Klaus Schwab, *The Global Competitiveness Report, 2016–2017* (Geneva: World Economic Forum, 2016), 47, http://www3.weforum.org/docs/GCR2016-2017/05FullReport/TheGlobalCompetitivenessReport2016-2017_FINAL.pdf.

7. American Society of Civil Engineers, "2017 Infrastructure Report Card: Economic Impact," https://www.infrastructurereportcard.org/the-impact/economic-impact/.

8. Lund et al., "Game Changers," 89.

9. David Allan Aschauer, "Is Public Expenditure Productive?," *Journal of Monetary Economics* 23, no. 2 (1989): 177–200; David Allan Aschauer, "Does Public Capital Crowd Out Private Capital?," *Journal of Monetary Economics* 24 (1989): 171–88; Alfredo M. Pereira and Jorge M. Andraz, "On the Economic Effects of Public Infrastructure Investment: A Survey of the International Evidence," *Journal of Economic Development* 38, no. 4 (2013): 1–37.

10. Claudia Copeland, Linda Levine, and William J. Mallett, "The Role of Public Works Infrastructure in Economic Recovery," Congressional Research Service, September 21, 2011, https://www.everycrsreport.com/reports/R42018.html.

11. Pereira and Andraz, "On the Economic Effects of Public Infrastructure Investment." In a study on highway capital spending, Leduc and Wilson find a positive effect of spending shocks on gross domestic product (GDP) during the first couple of years and then again about six to eight years later, but the effect disappeared by year ten. When they examined periods of economic recession versus expansion, they found that the initial effect was not observed during economic expansion but that the secondary effect appeared in both recessions and expansions. Sylvain Leduc and Daniel Wilson, "Are State Governments Roadblocks to Federal Stimulus? Evidence from Highway Grants in the 2009 Recovery Act," Federal Reserve Bank of San Francisco, Working Paper Series, Working Paper 2013-16, January 6, 2013, http://www.frbsf.org/economic-research/files/wp2013-16.pdf.

12. James Madison. *The Federalist Papers, No. 14: Objections to the Proposed Constitution from Extent of Territory Answered*, November 30, 1787, http://avalon.law.yale.edu/18th_century/fed14.asp.

13. Paul Johnson, *George Washington: The Founding Father* (New York: Harper-Collins Books, 2005).

14. Walter Isard, "A Neglected Cycle: The Transport Building Cycle," *Review of Economic Statistics* 24 (1942): 149–58.

15. Cranmer notes that the public share is underestimated since some projects that received both public and private funds were counted as private because the breakdown of the funding was not available. H. Jerome Cranmer, "Canal Investment, 1815–1860," in *Trends in the American Economy in the Nineteenth Century*, Studies in Income and Wealth, vol. 24, National Bureau of Economic Research (Princeton, NJ: Princeton University Press, 1960), http://www.nber.org/chapters/c2489.pdf.

16. National Park Service, "Erie Canal: History and Culture," February 26, 2015, https://www.nps.gov/erie/learn/historyculture/index.htm.

17. Henry C. Adams, *Public Debts: An Essay on the Science of Finance* (New York: D. Appleton, 1982), https://ia600200.us.archive.org/21/items/cu31924032556429/cu31924032556429.pdf, 304.

18. About thirty-five years later, during the depression of 1873, about 20 percent of all municipal debt was involved in or affected by a default. This led to additional constraints imposed on the issuance of debt. A. M. Hillhouse, *Municipal Bonds: A Century of Experience* (New York: Prentice Hall, 1936), 16.

19. Albert Gallatin, *Report of the Secretary of the Treasury, on the Subject of Public Roads and Canals; Made in Pursuance of a Resolution of the Senate, of March 2, 1807* (Washington, DC: R. C. Weightman, 1808), http://oll.libertyfund.org/titles.

20. Gayle Martinelli, "Albert Gallatin and Canals," https://www.nps.gov/articles/albert-gallatin-and-canals.htm.

21. Carter Goodrich, *Government Promotion of American Canals and Railroads, 1800–1890* (Westport, CT: Greenwood Press, 1960), 267–71.

22. James E. Vance Jr., *Capturing the Horizon: The Historical Geography of Transportation since the Transportation Revolution of the Sixteenth Century* (New York: Harper & Row, 1986), 304–18.

23. Lloyd Mercer, *Railroads and Land Grant Policy: A Study in Government Intervention* (New York: Academic Press, 1982), 3.

24. Goodrich, *Government Promotion*, 269.

25. Ibid., 270–71.

26. *The Secret Diary of Harold L. Ickes: The First Thousand Days, 1933–1936* (New York: Simon and Schuster, 1953), 78.

27. National Park Service, "Civilian Conservation Corps," https://www.nps.gov/thro/learn/historyculture/civilian-conservation-corps.htm.

28. Perry Merrill, *Roosevelt's Forest Army: A History of the Civilian Conservation Corps* (Montpellier, VT: Perry H. Merrill, 1981), 9.

29. Robert D. Leighninger, *Long-Range Public Investment: The Forgotten Legacy of the New Deal* (Columbia: University of South Carolina Press, 2007), 12.

30. Ibid., 38, 41.

31. Public Works Administration, *America Builds: The Record of PWA* (Washington, DC: Government Printing Office, 1939), 37, 53–55.

32. Howard Rosen, "Public Works: The Legacy of the New Deal," *Social Education* 60, no. 5 (1996): 278, http://www.socialstudies.org/sites/default/files/publications/se/6005/600506.html.

33. Public Works Administration, *America Builds*, 191.

34. Leighninger, *Long-Range Public Investment*, 37, 82–83.

35. Rosen, "Public Works," 278.

36. Leighninger, *Long-Range Public Investment*, 70.

37. Ibid., 61.

38. George H. Field, *Final Report on the WPA Program, 1935–43* (Washington, DC: Government Printing Office, 1946), http://lcweb2.loc.gov/service/gdc/scd0001/2008/20080212001fi/20080212001fi.pdf, 1.

39. Frank Freidel, "Panel Presentations," in *The New Deal Fifty Years After: A Historical Assessment*, ed. Wilbur J. Cohen (Austin: University of Texas Press, 1984), 77.

40. Dan McNichol, *The Incredible Story of the U.S. Interstate System: The Roads That Built America* (New York: Sterling, 2006), 26.

41. Elena S. Prassas and Roger P. Roess, *Engineering Economics and Finance for Transportation Infrastructure* (New York City: Springer, 2013), 155.

42. Vance, *Capturing the Horizon*, 171.

43. Stuart Bruchey, *The Roots of American Economic Growth, 1607–1861* (New York: Harper & Row, 1965), 124–40.

44. Prassas and Roess, *Engineering Economics and Finance*, 155.

45. McNichol, *Incredible Story of the U.S. Interstate System*, 19.

46. *Gibbons v. Ogden*, 22 U.S. 1 (1824); *Wilson v. Shaw*, 204 U.S. 24 (1907).

47. Prassas and Roess, *Engineering Economics and Finance*, 156.

48. McNichol, *Incredible Story of the U.S. Interstate System*, 59, 71.

49. Prassas and Roess, *Engineering Economics and Finance*, 159.

50. The official title of the report was *General Location of National System of Interstate Highways Including All Additional Routes at Urban Areas Designated in September 1955.*

51. Richard F. Weingroff, "Essential to the National Interest," *Public Roads* 69, no. 5 (2006).

52. Dwight Eisenhower, *Annual Message on the Economic Report*, January 24, 1956, http://www.presidency.ucsb.edu/ws/index.php?pid=10582.

53. Prassas and Roess, *Engineering Economics and Finance*, 160.

54. Weingroff, "Essential to the National Interest," 2006.

55. Earl Swift, *The Big Roads: The Untold Story of the Engineers, Visionaries, and Trailblazers Who Created the American Superhighways* (Boston: Mariner Books, Houghton Mifflin Harcourt, 2011), 314, 317.

56. Ibid., 229, 242.

57. Weingroff, "Essential to the National Interest," 10.

58. Swift, *Big Roads*, 306.

59. U.S. Department of Transportation, Federal Highway Administration and Federal Transit Administration, *2015 Status of the Nation's Highways, Bridges, and Transit: Conditions & Performance*, Publication FHWA-PL-17-002 (Washington, DC: Government Printing Office, 2017).

60. Federal Highway Administration, "Highway History," https://www.fhwa.dot.gov/interstate/faq.cfm#question1.

61. "America's Interstate Highways: America's Splurge," *Economist* (February 14, 2008), http://www.economist.com/node/10697196.

62. U.S. Department of Transportation, Federal Highway Administration and Federal Transit Administration, *2015 Status of the Nation's Highways, Bridges, and Transit.*

63. Toni Horst et al., "40 Proposed U.S. Transportation and Water Infrastructure Projects of Major Economic Significance," AECOM in Partnership with Compass Transportation, Inc., and Raymond Ellis Consulting, 2016, https://www.treasury.gov/connect/blog/Documents/final-infrastructure-report.pdf.

64. National Conference of State Legislatures, "Autonomous Vehicles/Self-Driving Vehicles Enacted Legislation," July 25, 2017, http://www.ncsl.org/research/transportation/autonomous-vehicles-self-driving-vehicles-enacted-legislation.aspx.

65. R. Richard Geddes and Thomas J. Madison Jr., "Fixing America's Roads and Bridges: The Path Forward," Committee for Economic Development of the Conference Board, 2017, https://www.ced.org/reports/single/fixing-americas-roads-bridges.

66. Tony Dutzik and Phineas Baxandall, "A New Direction: Our Changing Relationship with Driving and the Implications for America's Future," U.S. PIRG Education Fund and Frontier Group, 2013, http://www.uspirg.org/sites/pirg/files/reports/A%20New%20Direction%20vUS.pdf; "Millennials Embrace Ride-Hailing to Pave a New Path for Mobility," 2016, https://www.reportlinker.com/insight/mobility-services.html.

67. Serena Lei, "Meeting the Transportation Needs of an Aging Population," Urban Institute, 2013, http://www.urban.org/urban-wire/meeting-transportation-needs-aging-population.

68. Horst et al., "40 Proposed U.S. Transportation and Water Infrastructure Projects."

69. Rosen, "Public Works," 2.

70. American Society of Civil Engineers, "2017 Infrastructure Report Card."

71. The Congressional Budget Office also found that the overall net benefits could be increased by reallocating a substantial portion of the federal interstate and other federal-aid road funding from rural to urban areas. Congressional Budget Office, "Approaches to Make Federal Highway Spending More Productive," February 2016, www.cbo.gov/publications/50150, 25.

72. Michael Pagano, "Funding and Investing in Infrastructure," Urban Institute, 2011, http://www.urban.org/sites/default/files/publication/24996/412481-Funding-and-Investing-in-Infrastructure.PDF.

73. Federal Highway Administration, "Highway History."

74. Claudia Copeland, Steven Maguire, and William J. Mallett, "Legislative Options in the 114th Congress for Financing Water Infrastructure," Congressional Research Service, December 30, 2016, https://fas.org/sgp/crs/misc/R42467.pdf.

75. U.S. Government Accountability Office, "State Revolving Funds: Improved Financial Indicators Could Strengthen EPA Oversight, GAO 15-567," August 2015, https://www.gao.gov/assets/680/671855.pdf.

76. Copeland, Maguire, and Mallett, "Legislative Options in the 114th Congress."

77. U.S. Department of Housing and Urban Development, Office of Economic Resilience, Financing High-Performance Infrastructure, n.d., https://www.hudexchange.info/resources/documents/Financing-High-Performance-Infrastructure.pdf.

78. American Society of Civil Engineers, "2017 Infrastructure Report Card: Wastewater," https://www.infrastructurereportcard.org/wastewater/.

79. Local governments are increasingly using broadband technology to communicate with citizens during heavy rains or natural disasters. But for this approach to be effective, broadband needs to be accessible to all citizens. In 2016 10 percent of Americans (34 million people) lacked access to broadband with adequate speeds. Rural areas are more adversely impacted than urban areas (39 percent of the population in rural areas lack access compared to 4 percent of the population in urban areas). Federal Communication Commission, "2016 Broadband Progress Report," January 29, 2016, https://www.fcc.gov/reports-research/reports/broadband-progress-reports/2016-broadband-progress-report.

80. According to the National Conference of State Legislatures, since 2013 twenty-six states have passed legislation to increase the state motor-fuel taxes. National Conference of State Legislatures, "Fuel Tax Legislation," July 19, 2017, http://www.ncsl.org/research/transportation/2013-and-2014-legislative-actions-likely-to-change-gas-taxes.aspx.

81. Robert S. Kirk, "Tolling U.S. Highways," Congressional Research Service, CRS Report no. R43575, 2016, https://fas.org/sgp/crs/misc/R43575.pdf.

82. Congressional Research Service, "The Federal Excise Tax on Motor Fuels and the Highway Trust Fund: Current Law and Legislative History," February 22, 2016, https://www.everycrsreport.com/files/20160222_RL30304_5c2edf255c0cf959bf2c8b39175a5e64f0aac7b5.pdf.

83. Congressional Budget Office, "Options for Reducing the Deficit, 2014 to 2023," 2013, https://www.cbo.gov/sites/default/files/cbofiles/attachments/44715-OptionsForReducingDeficit-3.pdf, option 31.

84. Ibid.

85. In a review of twenty-eight polls that asked about a mileage tax, the Mineta Transportation Institute found that none of the polls found the majority of respondents supported the tax and that only five had support above 40 percent. In a survey conducted by the Mineta Transportation Institute annually over the period 2011–15, support for a one-cent flat mileage tax has ranged from 19 percent (2013 and 2014) to 24 percent (2015). However, there was increased support of the mileage tax to 44 percent in 2015 if the rate varied depending on the level of pollution emitted by a vehicle. Asha Weinstein and Hilary Nixon, "What Do Americans Think about Federal Tax Options to Support Public Transit, Highways, and Local Streets and Roads? Results from Year Six of a National Survey," Mineta Transportation Institute at San José State University, Report 12-51, 2015, http://transweb.sjsu.edu/PDFs/research/1428-road-tax-public-opinion-poll-2015.pdf.

86. The FAST Act included $95 million for grants to states for demonstration projects that utilize a user-fee structure. In the past, most pilot studies have been relatively small and addressed one particular locality or state. Recently, a pilot study with a mileage tax has been approved for the I-95 Corridor in Pennsylvania and Delaware. Robert S. Kirk and Marc Levinson, "Mileage-Based Road User Charges," Con-

gressional Research Service, CRS Report no. R44540, June 22, 2016, https://fas.org/sgp/crs/misc/R44540.pdf.

87. Simon Workman and Haime Rall, "Toll Facilities in the United States," National Conference of State Legislatures, February 1, 2013, http://www.ncsl.org/research/transportation/toll-facilities-in-the-united-states.aspx.

88. Jim Watts, "Infrastructure Proposals in Trump's Fiscal 2018 Budget and Fact Sheet Could Reduce Funding," *Bond Buyer* (May 25, 2017).

89. Kirk, "Tolling U.S. Highways."

90. National League of Cities, "NLC Resolution #423: Preserving the Tax-Exempt Status of Municipal Bonds," 2017 National League of Cities National Municipal Policy and Resolutions, Pittsburgh City Summit, November 19, 2016, http://www.nlc.org/sites/default/files/2016-12/2017%20National%20Municipal%20Policy%20Book_0.pdf.

91. U.S. Department of the Treasury, "Treasury Analysis of Build America Bonds Issuance and Savings," May 16, 2011, https://www.treasury.gov/initiatives/recovery/Documents/BABs%20Report.pdf.

92. Congressional Budget Office/Joint Committee on Taxation, "Subsidizing Infrastructure Investment with Tax-Preferred Bonds," October 2009, https://www.cbo.gov/publication/41359.

93. The subsidy on the Build America Bonds became subject to federal budget sequestration.

94. William A. Galston and Korin Davis, "Setting Priorities, Meeting Needs: The Case for a National Infrastructure Bank," Governance Studies at Brookings, December 13, 2013, https://www.brookings.edu/wp-content/uploads/2016/06/1213_infrastructure_galston_davis.pdf.

95. Emilia Istrate and Robert Puentes, "Investing for Success: Examining a Federal Capital Budget and a National Infrastructure Bank," Metropolitan Policy Program at Brookings, https://www.brookings.edu/wp-content/uploads/2016/06/1210_infrastructure_puentes.pdf.

96. World Bank, "Public-Private Partnerships Reference Guide," version 3, 2017, https://pppknowledgelab.org/guide/sections/83-what-is-the-ppp-reference-guide.

97. Justin Marlowe, "Municipal Bonds and Infrastructure Development—Past, Present, and Future," International City/County Management Association and Government Finance Officers Association, https://icma.org/sites/default/files/307554_15-08%20Municipal%20Bonds%20and%20Infrastructure%20Development_web%20updated.pdf.

98. Mary E. Peters and Samara Barend, "The Benefits of Private Financing for Public Works," *New York Times*, July 17, 2017, https://www.nytimes.com/2017/07/17/opinion/the-benefits-of-private-financing-for-public-works.html.

99. Ibid.

100. U.S. Government Accountability Office, "Highway Public-Private Partnerships: More Rigorous Up-Front Analysis Could Better Secure Potential Benefits

and Protect the Public Interest," GAO-08-44, February 2008, http://www.gao.gov/new.items/d0844.pdf.

101. Rudin Center for Transportation Policy and Management, "Maximizing the Value of New York's Investment in Public Construction: The Role of Design-Build Procurement," New York University, 2015, https://wagner.nyu.edu/impact/research/role-design-build-procurement.

102. Beverly Bunch, "Preserving the Public Interest in Highway Public-Private Partnerships: A Case Study of the State of Texas," *Public Budgeting & Finance* 32, no. 1 (2012): 36–57; U.S. Government Accountability Office, "Highway Public-Private Partnerships."

103. See U.S. Department of Transportation, Federal Highway Administration, "Center for Innovative Finance Support," https://www.fhwa.dot.gov/ipd/.

104. Emilia Istrate and Robert Puentes, "Moving Forward on Public Private Partnerships: U.S. and International Experience with PPP Units," Brookings-Rockefeller Project on State and Metropolitan Innovation, December 2011, https://www.brookings.edu/wp-content/uploads/2016/06/1208_transportation_istrate_puentes.pdf.

105. Joan Lowy and David A. Lieb, "Trump Advisers' Tax Credit Plan for Infrastructure Has Risks," *PBS Newshour*, February 7, 2017, http://www.pbs.org/newshour/rundown/trump-advisers-tax-credit-plan-infrastructure-risks/.

The Built Environment

How Infrastructure Shapes City Design Today and Tomorrow

SANJEEV VIDYARTHI

Great cities such as Chicago and *hard infrastructure*, or the investment in fixed assets designed to improve both the economic development opportunities and the physical design of cities, have a close, even if sometimes estranged, relationship. On the one hand, both give rise to each other, especially when the built environment (places, buildings, and open areas) and enabling infrastructure (facilities, utilities, public works, and more) are conceived and built complementarily. On the other hand, urban places and supporting infrastructure can quickly turn out of sync, leading to dysfunction and even disasters.[1] Dystopian chronicles of disinvestment in city infrastructure for a variety of reasons such as official neglect, social divide, and economic rifts in erstwhile productive places like Flint, Michigan, document such disasters in horrifying detail.[2]

Not surprisingly, real as well as perceived gaps between the features of the built environment and elements of hard infrastructure generate dissonance and vigorous public debate, while some of the biggest budget battles, irrespective of the geographical location and political leaning of the legislature or city hall, routinely concern infrastructure. Such a preoccupation with the nature and status of hard infrastructure across urban America is equally evident in the broad litany of complaints sponsors, planners, and builders of physical infrastructure face on an ongoing basis: design mismatch, bureaucratic tardiness, turf wars, petty politicking, talking past each other, working at cross-purposes, cost overruns, inordinate delays, boosterism, or unabashed promotion of a place in public perception for narrow economic gains often centered around showcase design projects and prestigious real estate developments. So how do we make sense of such a deeply intertwined relationship between hard infrastructure and city design? What is our experience, and what have we learned?

It is plain to see that cities cannot exist without hard infrastructure. Cities and physical infrastructure have always coexisted, with mutual interdependence and coevolution long characterizing their intimate relationship. In fact, an important strand of urban historiography views modern cities as completely man-made entities that emerged from the interaction of society and technology because neither economic development nor urbanization could have occurred without the creation of enabling infrastructure.[3] In this line of thinking, infrastructure leads city development (especially in developed societies) by getting built first and then continuing to shape urban growth for a long time because of its foundational and enduring nature—easily outliving many other urban elements, like built and open spaces, by decades and even centuries.[4]

It is equally clear that the roles and significance of physical infrastructure have increased dramatically since the advent of large modern metropolises in the late nineteenth century, and as a postindustrial society today we are more dependent on technology-enabled infrastructures than at any time in the past.[5] Moreover, as cities compete at the global level, leaders recognize the critical role of infrastructure in creating high-quality urban facilities and living environments that provide crucial competitive advantage.[6] Contemporary trends presaging the planet's increasingly urban future, including the emergence of megacities, massive urban regions, and the networking of places and communities, all rely on infrastructures.[7] Moreover, governments remain fixated on infrastructure for a variety of reasons, such as society's overall development, administrative control of populations, and bolstering economic growth.[8] For instance, President Barack Obama's Recovery Act of 2009, despite the ongoing neoliberal impulses in this country, aimed at using investment in hard infrastructure to boost economic activity.

Not surprisingly, literature tracks the development of various forms and elements of hard infrastructure in shaping modern cities from a variety of positions and perspectives.[9] In this chapter, I offer a brief overview, summarizing key insights from this extensive literature toward illustrating the nexus between hard infrastructure and city design in order to highlight key lessons for designing the cities of tomorrow.

CONCEIVING HARD INFRASTRUCTURE

Even though urban physical infrastructure seems to be a moving target, resisting precise specification, many scholarly conceptions and definitions refer to fixed assets in the form of built facilities and networks, either below or over ground, which support human health, safety, and welfare.[10] More important, the term's meaning has continued to expand over time, largely to include a growing number of different systems. For instance, the focus has grown to include a range of publicly and privately owned providers of spatial systems enabling and supporting human life in modern urban environments, such as utilities (gas and electricity, water supply and sewerage, waste collection and disposal), public works (roads and bridges, dams and canals, ports and airports, railways and multimodal transportation hubs), community facilities (schools, parks, hospitals, libraries, and prisons), and telecommunications (telephone, cable television, and the Internet). Given their significance for modern urban life, many of these systems are nowadays termed critical infrastructure.[11]

While networks are clearly a part of this complex arrangement undergirding contemporary city life, often the policy and implementation focus has been on a single project (for example, the widening of I-290), facility (building a new pumping station), or a public work (rebuilding Lower Wacker Drive). Moreover, within these efforts, emphasis has customarily focused on a specific aspect, such as the nuts and bolts of physical configuration, compared to other ramifications like the larger meaning and value addition generated by different networks constituting hard infrastructure.[12]

Michael Neuman and Sherri Smith argue that such a narrow focus stems from the emergence of many professions (rather than one single profession) developing expertise in different domains of urban infrastructure, such as transportation, electric supply, telecommunications, and municipal administration.[13] With each profession focused on its own specialized domain, it is not surprising that a plethora of definitions explaining hard infrastructure exist that are largely in line with the specific expertise of that particular profession and frequently codified in relevant professional norms and statutory rules and instruments. Neuman identifies different professions (identified in parentheses) that have proffered categorical denominations suited to their disciplines, such as utilities (service providers), urban infrastructure (city planning), public works (civil engineering), capital facilities (business administration), capital investments (finance), community facilities (public administration), and civic improvements (architecture). Digging deeper into these categories provides a good idea about how different professions and concerned authorities have conceived and organized the various components of hard infrastructure across space and time.[14]

Utilities refer to an important subcategory of infrastructure financed largely by user fees, mostly administered locally in specified geographies, and delivered directly to the user premises. Water supply, waste collection, electricity, and natural gas are common types of utilities. Historically also known as public utilities, many utility companies have either private or public owners and little or no competition in their service areas. But the utility market landscape is increasingly changing, characterized both by growing competition and by concomitant regulatory supervision for consumer protection. In contrast, the term *public works* commonly refers to an individual large-scale facility customarily imposing no direct charge on the users that is usually built by the public sector for the benefit of the general public. Examples include dams, reservoirs, ports, bridges, roads, and airports—almost all of which belong exclusively to the domain of public-sector construction. Today, the term *public works* continues to connote large-scale engineering projects even as prevalent ideas about user charges and fees have begun to change.[15]

Associated with the City Beautiful movement, the term *city improvement* emerged around the turn of the nineteenth century to refer to public projects targeted at bettering the overall built environment for the benefit of city residents. In line with the tenets of the Progressive Era, examples include the building of useful and prominent public facilities such as libraries, city halls, parks, boulevards, public lighting, and street furniture. Designed by well-known architects and landscape designers, these projects also aimed at instilling civic pride by improving the urban environment that had become filthy and crowded in the industrial era. Today the term *civic improvement* generally refers to the (re)design of urban spaces through built projects encompassing more functional infrastructures than the City Beautiful predecessors, such as marinas, ports, and public transit.[16]

The term *community facility* includes buildings such as city halls, fire and police stations, parks, libraries, and schools meant to serve a specific set of users (individual community) at a particular scale (municipal or neighborhood). Usually owned and operated by the public sector, they were called public facilities in the recent past. In the wake of ongoing privatization, the relatively generic term *community facilities privileging scale to ownership* has gained currency. In the case of small communities and private subdivisions, some of these facilities are provided by citizen volunteers, such as firefighters, and others may be provided privately, such as a swimming pool and community center, by a home owners' association.

The notion of investing financial capital into an individual facility lies at the heart of the term *capital facilities*. The focus on a particular facility is common with the term *public works*, but capital facilities can be owned by private, public, nonprofit, or mixed ownership. Originally connoting initial investment into any large public facility or network that performs a service to its users and owners, the term *capital facilities* has gradually expanded to include one of the broadest classifications of infrastructure, encompassing libraries, schools, community facilities, and even utilities. Although closely related, the term *capital investment* explicitly emphasizes the role of financial capital in infrastructure development and the return on investment anticipated by the investors. Neuman argues that in practice, however, this is largely an accounting issue with local variations and is not injurious to the overall concept of infrastructure as a capital investment.[17]

But even as different professions conceptualize infrastructure into various categories in line with their professional expertise, different conceptions and interpretations can easily impede mutual understanding and coordination because many elements of infrastructure frequently overlap and connect with each other. In the category of capital investments, for instance, policy makers, decision makers, and investors think and operate in terms of loans, interest rates, debt ratios, and satisfying relevant constituencies with specific projects. In the realm of public works, engineers employ a set of tools and ideas substantially dissimilar to that of policy makers. In the domain of community facilities and transportation, the same can be said about urban planners, architects, and landscape architects, who both design and site infrastructure into the existing urban fabric as well as plan new development patterns. As a result, decisions are routinely made piecemeal, with the inevitable high costs and consequences of the attendant lack of coordination. This fairly ubiquitous phenomenon not only brings blame to the doors of planners and builders of infrastructure but also predicates a major critique of the manner in which we have customarily conceived and built various elements of hard infrastructure.[18]

The second (and in fact a much older) critique comes from scholars studying the social and environmental implications of hard infrastructure and its physical design. Critiquing the underlying spatially centered perspective that assumes social problems can be solved by manipulating the physical built environment, scholars like Herbert Gans describe how spatial solutions are not a prerequisite to thriving social communities, at least not to the extent posited by the advocates of hard infrastructure.[19] Along similar lines, William Sherman describes how the modern predilection for large-scale spatial solutions that sought to insulate human communities from the vagaries of nature not only portended growing disengagement with the surrounding natural environment but also shaped the nature and meaning of design itself in fundamental ways:

For the past hundred years . . . the incessant search for new form has been supported by the evolving technological apparatus of modernity. The process of abstraction that characterizes modern thought finds a physical analog in the vast infrastructures created to parallel and stabilize dynamic ecological systems. These infrastructural systems replace the temporal processes and spatial limits of a tangible place, allowing discrete works of design to disengage from their local surround. As a result, these projects stand seemingly absolved from accounting for their cultural and ecological impacts. The essential processes that structure human engagements with the physical world have been reduced to a resource delivery system, reflecting a predilection rooted in modernity for the ravenous consumption of the present tense, with-out consequence beyond the moment. The long-term impact of our technologically driven, consumer culture necessitates a critical reconsideration of the failings of this modern apparatus as a precondition for design.[20]

Informed both by these critiques and by the growing scope and significance of hard infrastructure in enabling and sustaining modern city life, recent scholarship has begun paying attention to the larger meaning and value addition generated by different networks constituting hard infrastructure. Neuman, for example, has argued that infrastructure does not simply lie underneath other structures, such as buildings or cities, but brings life and connects them in meaningful ways. Infrastructure is deliberately designed to infuse vitality, channeling a range of critical utilities (water, energy, people, information, wastes, and commodities) across different components of each supported building. It then links these buildings intelligibly with nearby places and facilities and, at still larger spatial scales, physically creates both the individual parts and the overall network of human settlements. This new understanding, based on a reconception of the nature of infrastructures, reflects how infrastructures infiltrate human habitats rather than underlie obscurely.[21] In this sense, hard infrastructure is the "connective tissue that knits people, places, social institutions and natural environment into coherent urban relations."[22]

Adding value to places and buildings then is the fundamental nature and purpose of contemporary infrastructure. These value additions gain special significance in large cities and urban regions due to different kinds of densities and intensities at play among various infrastructure networks. The network of networks is more closely woven in cities due to the spatial proximity of various buildings and places (or nodes are closer together), generating efficiencies and more benefit to the users. But unanticipated interactions among spatially proximate infrastructures can also entail negative costs to both users and nonusers. Informed by such an expansive understanding based on infrastructure network theory, Neuman offers the following broad definition of infrastructure:

> Infrastructure is the physical network that channels a flux (water, fluid, electricity, energy, material, people, digital signal, analog signal etc.) through conduits (tubes, pipes, canals, channels, roads, rails, wires, cables, fibers, lines etc.) or a medium (air, water) with the purpose of supporting a human population, usually located in a settlement, for the general or common good. It consists of a long-lasting network connecting producers and service providers with a large number of users through standardized (while variable) technologies, pricing and controls that are planned and managed by coordinating organizations.[23]

How did we reach such a capacious conception of hard infrastructure?

CHANGING IDEAS ABOUT HARD INFRASTRUCTURE

This is not the first study of the relationship between hard infrastructure and city design. I describe here some of the extensive literature mainly to frame the context for judging and distilling important insights and lessons for designing better cities than the past. Before doing so, however, the following two backstories help comprehend the overall nature and disposition of the American planning tradition that scaffolds the relationship between physical design of places and infiltrating infrastructures in important ways.

First, in a brilliant essay overviewing the American planning tradition over the past couple of centuries, leading urban historian Robert Fishman explains how national planning played a crucial role in the rapid creation of a continent-size urban order by focusing on large-scale infrastructural elements such as transcontinental railroads, great hydroelectric dams of the South and West, and the interstate highway system. Arguing that the "federal government itself was created in large part to overcome the barriers to national planning that existed under the Articles of Confederation," he posits that "no other nation has been so profoundly *planned* as the United States."[24] Countering the widely popular narrative in this country that national planning is an un-American activity—an exercise in bureaucratic hubris best left to the French—the essay goes on to illustrate the unique nature and structure of the American planning system.

According to Fishman, the remarkable power of planning in the United States is proportional to the strengths of the impediments it must constantly overcome. These obstacles include powerful ideas and structural elements such as the centrality of private property and the influence of this notion over important domains like economic thought and material culture and the federal system of government with its complex division of powers. Planning in this country has therefore always been innovative and opportunistic, exploiting the flexibility in the federal system to bypass opposition while constantly seeking new coalitions of stakeholders that can advance the goals.

For instance, depending on the issue at hand, the stakeholder coalition can easily include diverse players from an impressive spectrum of planning actors, such as federal or state agencies, public-sector organizations, private institutions, individual entrepreneurs, local politicians, members of the civil society, property developers, and even real estate speculators. This special characteristic of American planning, where despite the lack of top-down bureaucracies to conduct planning (such as those in France and other European countries), the relatively open American system not only encourages citizen activism but also fosters close cooperation between seemingly incompatible stakeholders, such as progressive leaders, real estate builders, and staunch environmentalists. Importantly, the federal system, with its division of power between the national government and states and constituent urban regions and settlements of varying size and function, provides unexpected strength and a diverse range of practical opportunities to conduct planning at different spatial and policy scales. Thus, any study of planning work (conceiving, predicting, designing, composing, implementation) involving hard infrastructure and city design in this country must pay attention to cross-scalar interactions between relevant policy domains and spatial realms shaped by the political dynamic and (often unique) contexts and cultures of local places and specific settlements.

The second, and interrelated with the previous, backstory describes the long-term development of the relationship between infrastructure provisioning and the field of urban planning in the United States. In a series of well-articulated essays, leading subject expert Michael Neuman has illustrated the relationship's nonlinear nature while describing the major historic episodes that shaped the nexus.[25] He describes how the connections between modern infrastructure planning and city design were intimately intertwined at the beginning of the relationship during the last quarter of the nineteenth century, and although the links remain numerous and multifaceted, the relationship today is mostly nonstrategic and noncomprehensive, even as the bond between infrastructures and cities remains tight. Scholars tracking other domains of infrastructure planning confirm Neuman's thesis.

Take the example of road infrastructure, for instance, where Michael Fein identifies major policy regimes that have shaped the history of road building in New York State.[26] Beginning in the late nineteenth century, local communities organized the entire wherewithal to plan and build the few primitive roads that existed at the time but always paid close attention to road alignment and its integration with settlements' physical layouts and foreseeable spatial futures. The second policy regime emerged around the turn of the century when some, albeit largely urban, interests began to turn toward the state of New York in an effort to build more and better roads. Local officials' volunteer cooperation with higher authorities helped access state funds for building better roads through adjacent locales—despite many and long-standing differences that often marked their relationship. Many of these roads, however, also opened city edges and peripheral areas for building new urban extensions and designing real estate projects. Local interests, however, still shaped decision making around road location and alignment but now generated many more potential opportunities for political patronage and actual corruption, as the size and scope of roadwork increased substantially.

Shortly afterward, emergence of the new profession of highway engineers accompanied the employment of progressive language of efficiency and technical expertise. This shift helped professionals pursue administrative and procedural reforms and gradually gain control of the road-building process from local and often vested interests. Increasingly asserting the superiority of their supposedly nonpolitical approach, engineers' efforts culminated in the creation of a state highway department that they headed. Seeing the value in deflecting criticism from the legislature, politicians then ceded authority to the highway department and its engineers while retaining oversight control.

The New Deal ushered in the next policy regime that saw greater federal money and involvement. Fein argues that during this period, federal and state governments negotiated a power-sharing arrangement, even as the states further insulated the road-building process from voters and local interests with the creation of an independent public authority to plan, finance, and build the New York State Thruway. Importantly, he shows that the movement of power and control from the local to state to national level was a nonlinear process that was highly contested at almost every stage. States did not simply cede control with the advent of federal funding; rather, the road-building process became a cooperative venture with substantial state and mayoral influence over when and where roads and, particularly, the interstate system would be built—an arrangement that shaped the spatial design and physical layout of postwar American cities and settlements in profound ways.

THE CENTRALIZATION-DECENTRALIZATION DEBATE

Since the planning and provisioning of hard infrastructure commonly entail thinking and working across multiple policy domains and different political jurisdictions, the questions of relevant scale and the nature and scope of effort assume considerable significance. Even as professionals tend to support large-scale centralized systems, for ostensibly important reasons such as supervisory coordination and control and efficiencies of various kinds, influential actors such as place-based voters and community leaders often espouse decentralized distribution of power, preferring local control over elements of infrastructure within their jurisdictions. Attendant debates about the size and role of government and the scope of regulatory controls, especially in this country, shape this dynamic as well. Not surprisingly, this broader debate between the advocates of decentralized control and centralized power has long influenced the nature of planning, shaping the relationship between city design and hard infrastructure in critical ways.

Historically, however, city design has been deeply rooted in infrastructure planning. Before the advent of the modern planning era, usually attributed to the efforts of Georges Haussmann in Paris and Ildefons Cerdà in Barcelona around the middle of the nineteenth century, the physical design of cities was often conceived at the scale of communities (which were spatially small since the dominant mode of transport was walking) and customarily articulated in terms of infrastructure planning that included layout of streets, public squares, and open spaces as well as the location of monuments, churches, and markets. Physical infrastructure was the primary object of city design as well as the main vehicle for pursuing its realization.[27]

This paradigm changed with Haussmann, who was a skillful administrator tasked by the French royal court to improve mid-nineteenth-century Paris that had deteriorated on account of various reasons, such as industrialization, urbanization, and a lack of organized planning. He introduced the model of comprehensive city improvement through physical design conceived and implemented via centralized planning. By focusing on the creation of a modern network of wide boulevards, many of which cut through the existing urban fabric, and new roads connecting prominent civic monuments, his plan transformed large parts of Paris by creating sanitary infrastructure, street lighting, omnibuses, and open spaces, comprising two large parks and numerous community facilities, such as schools and hospitals. Perhaps most important, he embraced a design-oriented spatial view derived through a physical survey of the entire city that in turn helped integrate the impressive array of open spaces, civic amenities, and well-provisioned residential areas into an operative whole through a modern circulatory system.[28]

Cerdà advanced this line of thinking by expanding the scope of the survey (incorporating social, public health, housing, and the physical environment conditions as well), enhancing the focus of city planning and design to include outward-oriented development and a comparatively better provision of infrastructure than Haussmann. For example, using innovative studies exploring the spatial integration of public open areas and residential buildings for the design of housing blocks, his centrally conceived and executed plan envisaged Barcelona's first major extension beyond the city walls. A carefully designed civic infrastructure of public parks and plazas, roads and sidewalks, water supply, sewerage and storm drains, and multilevel transportation interchanges that foresaw urban mass transit not only characterized his seminal plan but also established the importance of infrastructure-oriented design thinking in the emergent field of modern city planning.[29]

Many of these ideas quickly transferred to the United States, exerting influence on the incipient field of urban planning that had begun to emerge on this side of the Atlantic as well.[30] None other than Frederick Law Olmsted, a founding figure of landscape architecture and city planning in the United States who also served as the director of the U.S. Sanitary Commission, transformed the retail practice of city planning—traditionally conducted through town layouts, focusing primarily on streets, lots, and squares—into a more carefully conceived spatial design–oriented craft, paying attention to parks, parkways, and landscaped open areas as well as sanitary infrastructure. Olmsted's 1868 plan for Riverside, Illinois, for instance, not only showcased these ideas in practice but also established a prototypical model for similar efforts in other cities.[31]

Landmark planning events, such as the Chicago Columbian Exposition of 1893 and Daniel Burnham and Edward Bennett's *Plan of Chicago*, published in 1909, further popularized the idea of comprehensive urban improvement through centrally planned spatial design interventions. Attracting new clientele such as downtown business owners, city boosters, and emergent urban middle classes, growth-inducing and growth-shaping infrastructural elements like waterfronts, street improvements, transportation, parks, and public open spaces soon rose high on the political agenda as well. Among other things, such as fomenting the professionalization of the planning discipline, the subsequent City Beautiful movement not only helped expand urban planning's focus from infrastructure and hygiene to political, administrative, and legal concerns but also enhanced the geographical focus from the municipal to a regional scale.[32] Both these developments had a profound influence on the relationship between hard infrastructure and city design.

On the one hand, as professional planning matured, it began to align with powerful economic institutions, such as the Chambers of Commerce, and political-administrative organizations, such as city halls. Not surprisingly, city planning's focus began to shift from city design–oriented infrastructure planning and urban aesthetic considerations to administration, control of land use and private property through zoning, and coping with the widespread use of motorcars. Urban historian Christine Boyer explains, "Out of the complex of infrastructural and service needs, [modern] city planning from its inception became a multi-faceted process." In the void created due to the shift in city planning, state-appointed public utilities or public services commissions stepped in and began taking control of infrastructure from the city governments.[33]

On the other hand, practitioners in the field increasingly recognized the regional scope and structure of the emergent modern metropolis. The *Regional Plan of New York and Its Environs*, prepared during the 1920s, first articulated the idea of regional planning. Documenting an increasingly urbanized population across twenty-two counties in three states, the plan posited a key tenet of the regional planning model: urban growth is best anticipated and guided at the metropolitan scale because the futures of adjacent settlements are tied together through shared economic and infrastructural (especially transportation and environmental) systems. Arguing that partisan interests weaken civic solidarity and limit public attention within narrow political borders, the plan's authors advocated state support for employing regional infrastructural systems as the operating framework while calling on local communities to cooperate rather than compete. Despite formidable opposition from conservative suburbanites and public-sector skeptics, the regional plan's progressivism shaped the New York region in important ways—albeit in a piecemeal fashion over several decades—casting a formative influence on both the discipline and the practice of planning, which grew exponentially in the postwar period.[34]

Using the benefit of hindsight, Fishman has identified *Regionalists* and *Metropolitanists* as two rival planning traditions that both consolidated in the 1920s and shaped the changing relationship between city design and infrastructure planning. True to their name, Regionalists advocated region-wide planning and thereby focused on issues like regional land uses, intergovernmental coordination, and infrastructure policy.[35] By extension, and even if implicitly, they did not accord high priority to the issues of city design and urban aesthetics that arguably mattered less at the regional scale.[36] Metropolitanists, in contrast, represented the dominant establishment view and believed that the giant metropolis of the future would still be defined by its downtown, "the overwhelming economic and cultural focus of the metropolitan area."[37]

Not surprisingly, Metropolitanists accorded relatively higher priority to city design, believing that the basic urban form of American cities established in the nineteenth century would persist. Most of the population would continue to cluster around a monumental downtown worthy of a great urban civilization in an improved and better-designed "factory zone," or the productive heart of the metropolis. Beyond this zone would be the residential suburbs, housing a relatively small urban elite, and then the "outer zone," containing farms, parks, and forests. Importantly, they believed that each of these zones could be carefully planned in line with modern ideas and prevalent design concepts, balancing the quality of city life and easy access to nature via transit lines and parkways.[38]

Between the 1920s and 1960s, however, two shifts in the Metropolitanist tradition, symbolized by Robert Moses's massive projects for New York, not only underscored the importance of, often unforeseen, planning challenges associated with building large-scale infrastructure projects in urban settings but also illustrated the significance of carefully choosing the appropriate scale of design intervention. First, in contrast with the pioneers of the Metropolitanist tradition, who had championed rail mass-transit investments to knit the region together, Moses and his followers believed in the total dominance of the automobile and set out to rebuild the city in line with this conviction. Second, they embraced urban renewal as a total solution to "urban blight," believing that only the complete leveling of whole neighborhoods followed by rebuilding using the design concept of the "tower in the park" could create a viable modern city.[39]

Although recent literature acknowledges the salience of Moses's contributions toward transforming New York into the modern global city that it is today,[40] the severe backlash to his modernist schemes at the time not only discredited the recently established disciplines of city planning and urban design but also advanced the fields' growing distance from infrastructure planning that had come to rely increasingly on "megaprojects," or "initiatives that are physical, very expensive and public," to revitalize cities and stimulate their economic growth. The influence of the growth-oriented metropolitan elite, however, had already begun to wane, even as new constraints requiring major alterations in design and mitigation strategies were about to massively drive up the cost of megaprojects, swiftly changing the overall character of urban politics during the late 1960s and early 1970s.[41]

In line with these shifts, the planning academe began to critique infrastructure planning and physical design from a social equity, community design, and place-based perspective while focusing on emergent factors such as the declining economic value of new highways (Paul Peterson), the growing minority share of the central-city electorate (Clarence Stone), and the increasing importance of civic amenities as a competitive asset (John R. Logan and Harvey Molotch). On the other hand, planning practice continued the gradual shift away from the physical form that had been a critical constituent of city planning in the United States.[42] Professional engineers, meanwhile, took over regional-scale infrastructure planning and provisioning using sizable federal funds and ideas about efficiencies as the guiding mantra.[43] Larger debates around the issues of social justice and environmental degradation that crystallized around the same time, however, gradually laid the foundation to rethink this arrangement through the last few decades of the previous century.

THE INFLUENCE OF LARGER DEBATES AND MOVEMENTS

Since design and planning work always take place within the broader armature of the sociopolitical climate and cultural disposition of the society, the influence of dominant social debates and intellectual movements is both wide and deep. Examples include progressive and urban reform movements and debates around centralization vis-à-vis decentralization of political power that critically shaped and transformed ideas and actions in the fields of city design and infrastructure planning. There was also an influence of movements around social justice and environmental issues over the relationship between city design and physical infrastructure. Gaining traction around the same time, when modernist plans and projects came under fire through the 1960s and early 1970s, these movements not only cast an ameliorating influence but have also arguably helped planners reimagine the estranged relationship between city design and infrastructure planning over time.

Influential writer-activists like Jane Jacobs and planners such as Paul Davidoff brought the issues around social equity and justice to the fore in the aftermath of urban renewal and urban expressways during the 1960s. Their writings were important not only because they critiqued infrastructure planning, led by transportation specialists and aided by federal and market subsidies, particularly in relation to low-income communities, but also because they ushered in a profound reconsideration of urban planning's meaning and purpose while casting a long-lasting influence on its literature and practice.

Davidoff's seminal article "Advocacy and Pluralism in Planning," for instance, illustrated the importance of giving voice to the underrepresented and advocating on their behalf in the planning arena. In a similar vein, Jane Jacobs highlighted the importance of local places and place-based communities for making lively cities and paying attention to fine-grained urbanism, particularly at the neighborhood level.[44] Although it took planners considerable time to translate these discursive ideas into mainstream practice, while recovering from the almost complete breakdown of the comprehensive planning ideal, concepts such as "place making," "public participation," "social equity," and fine-grained "mixed land uses" slowly became accepted planning wisdom, supported by popular design movements like the Congress of New Urbanism and adopted in major public sector programs such as HOPE VI.[45]

In the envisaged scheme, planners strive to engage local residents and relevant stakeholders in the process of designing local places and compatible projects (no noxious land uses and facilities in low-income communities, for instance), while paying attention to supporting physical infrastructure at the appropriate spatial scale (usually blocks and neighborhoods). Importantly, large-scale spatial interventions, often necessary for building major urban infrastructure projects (such as the recent redesigning of Chicago's Jane Byrne Interchange), remain largely in the purview of administrators and engineers of public works agencies, transportation departments, and budget or finance offices.[46]

In sharp contrast with the community-level and place-based focus of social equity–oriented planners, environmental advocates have arguably paid more attention to the larger spatial and policy scales of cities, states, and the nation. Calling for state intervention and support from the beginning, upper- and middle-class professionals led the environmental movement that grew as a political action movement in the 1960s and focused on government-sponsored policies and legislative actions aimed at reducing energy and material consumption, waste production, and their impacts on the physical environment. Gaining momentum with landmark federal legislation such as the Clean Air Act (1963), National Environmental Protection Act (1970), Clean Water Act (1972), and the Superfund (1980) and Oil Pollution Acts (1990), the environmental movement made steady progress in the last decades of the previous century.[47]

Not surprisingly, infrastructure lies at the core of many of environmentalists' concerns. In the United States, for example, according to the Department of

Energy, most energy is consumed by infrastructure use or the infrastructure system itself. Twenty-eight percent of all energy was used by the transportation sector, while residential, industrial, and commercial structures accounted for more than 50 percent in 2007. Moreover, urban areas consume energy and produce carbon dioxide at a rate disproportionate to their population, with estimates ranging from 60 percent to 75 percent for energy use worldwide compared to just 50 percent of the global population.[48] Thus, in order to reduce emissions and carbon dioxide production, getting infrastructure right is critical.

From an environmental perspective, two insights shaping contemporary thinking about the relationship between hard infrastructure and city design stand out. First, professionals increasingly realize the folly of relying solely on man-made infrastructural systems to service large urban areas. For example, Chicago's TARP (Tunnel and Reservoir Plan), one of the largest civil engineering projects ever undertaken in terms of scope, cost, and time frame, has clearly demonstrated our inability to safely dispose of all the storm water and sewerage, especially during hard-to-predict extreme-weather events.[49] Turning to design with nature (rather than control or dominance), planners and policy makers increasingly think around "green infrastructure," or the natural network of parks, rivers, open spaces, forests, and wetlands, for conceiving future-oriented resilient solutions that could purposefully combine the new green and existing hard infrastructure for supporting city life in the social-ecological systems of large (and still growing) urban areas.[50]

Second, and in line with Fishman's nuanced reading of the American planning tradition, professionals and local leaders consistently, even if tacitly, use the relatively open American planning system to innovate and take the lead in pursuing progressive planning ideas at the city and state levels. Notwithstanding the prevalent climate of political opinion at the federal level and broader changes in economic thought about the appropriate roles of public and private sectors in infrastructure financing and building, states like California and New Jersey, and cities like Portland and Gainesville, for instance, have steadily pursued environmentally friendly policies and plans over time.[51]

Even in the conservative state of Georgia, the two-term mayor of Atlanta Shirley Franklin, who called herself the "sewer mayor," unabashedly aligned her political agenda with infrastructure by providing leadership and organizing financing. With a 50 percent increase in property taxes and a 1 percent voter-approved sales tax dedicated to infrastructure, she set out to clean waterways and city sewers, bolster biking and walking, and, perhaps most important, link infrastructure with city planning through the innovative "BeltLine" project. An innovative economic development and sustainable urban redevelopment effort to link forty-five neighborhoods via a twenty-two-mile loop of multi-use trails, parks, and green transit corridors, the BeltLine is being developed on an abandoned railroad's right-of-way.[52] Indeed, riding high on the back of increasingly popular terms such as *sustainability* and *resilience* in policy and social discourses, the importance of planning better infrastructure and smarter local places than the past efforts can (and should) rise higher on the agenda of intellectual classes and progressive leaders.[53]

CONCLUSION

This chapter began by asking, what is our experience with infrastructure planning and city design, and what have we learned? As illustrated, the relationship between infrastructure planning and city design has always been close, even if estranged at times. Not discounting the importance of changing regimes and larger social influences, this chapter has suggested that the stronger the relationship between city design and infrastructure provision, the more the professional activity of city planning and indeed the cities themselves have benefited. The following are key insights and a set of prospective policies that cities and metropolitan regions ought to consider and analyze for possible implementation, exploring both the challenges and the benefits of such actions:

- Infrastructure provides a solid platform for leadership because residents pay attention to their quality of life. Diligent infrastructure planning coupled with careful design for local places can aid in solving vexing problems such as equitable access to civic amenities and facilities, promote sustainable urban development, and preserve rural and natural areas. Challenges to such an approach may include opposition from vested interests, lack of political momentum, or simply the absence of a suitable policy climate. Grassroots initiatives by local voters that are supported by advocacy and equity-oriented planners and spearheaded by progressive leaders can both help organize such efforts and tap diverse sources of support from federal and state agencies.

* Collaboration is the key to pursuing progressive policies and projects in order to maximize the cumulative gains from the nexus between cleverly conceptualized city-design solutions and complementing infrastructural systems. Planners, engineers, and other professionals have

all acknowledged that infrastructural issues in the complex contemporary world cannot be addressed by any single profession acting alone. But professionals, however united collectively, must act in concert with society and its progressive leaders to secure sustainable and lasting improvements. Challenges to such an approach may include professional rivalry and bureaucratic turf wars. The overarching and binding nature of contemporary infrastructure, however, can help bridge divides and promote meaningful collaboration.

- Owing to its centrality in sustaining contemporary city life, infrastructure can help herald a new kind of place- and people-centered city planning. Much of the planning's current toolbox (methods, techniques, and procedures) is inherited from the approaches deployed to enhance economic productivity and ameliorate the poor quality of human life in the industrial cities of the nineteenth century. Today, there is increasing recognition that contemporary cities and metropolitan regions are complex entities with nothing like them in the natural world. Professionals can help shift the paradigm to address new understandings by aligning emergent tools and inventive techniques (for example, life-cycle planning, combined risk and cost-benefit analysis, and community-centered design charrette) with money and power—the domain of politics and finance and makers of infrastructure decisions—while paying attention to the values of sustainability, social equity, and environmental integrity, along with the field's original concerns around health, safety, and welfare.

  For instance, life-cycle planning, or a responsive approach considering the consequences (both on demand and supply side) over the lifetime of various project components, while contextualizing technical and monetary considerations along with environmental, social, and other criteria as part of the decision-making processes, can help ensure that planning is long term, comprehensive, and sustainable.[54] Moreover, such an approach can help all of the concerned disciplines, like city planning, public policy, urban design, and environmental engineering, work together while co-conceiving solutions that meet cultural, spatial, and temporal considerations specific to particular places and project clientele. Employing a combined risk and cost-benefit analysis can similarly help professionals include a focus on different kinds of risk and analyses of uncertainties, such as those associated with depleting resources and climate change, as they conceive and analyze new projects. Further along the policy and spatial analysis continuum, use of a community-centered design charrette can facilitate the hands-on engagement of professionals with place-based communities at the much more intimate scale of specific locales than the traditional "top-down" interventions.

Although many people and positions routinely perceive different facets and consequences of infrastructure and city design in an isolated manner, owing to a variety of reasons such as divergent worldviews, jurisdictional fidelity, and ideological commitments, the scholarly literature has begun to acknowledge that their intimately intertwined relationship holds an important key to the future sustainability of city life on this planet. As illustrated in this chapter, an increasing body of empirical and interdisciplinary knowledge can help professionals and progressive leaders move toward a new paradigm centered on codesigning and cobuilding sustainable, safe, secure, pleasing, and inclusive human settlements—impossible to conceive, build, or maintain without supporting infrastructure systems. Diverse challenges associated with any major shift in the "normal way of doing business" may pose challenges to such an approach, but growing awareness about the centrality of infrastructure to modern city life can help move forward.

Notes

1. Stephen Graham and Simon Marvin, *When Infrastructure Fails* (New York: Routledge, 2001).

2. Dora Apel, *Beautiful Terrible Ruins: Detroit and the Anxiety of Decline* (New Brunswick, NJ: Rutgers University Press, 2015); Andrew R. Highsmith, *Demolition Means Progress: Flint, Michigan, and the Fate of the American Metropolis* (Chicago: University of Chicago Press, 2015).

3. Joel Tarr, "The Evolution of Urban Infrastructure in the Nineteenth and Twentieth Centuries," in *Perspectives on Urban Infrastructure*, ed. Royce Hanson (Washington, DC: National Academy Press, 1984).

4. Literature documents the paucity of infrastructure in many parts of the world, where its provision often trails human habitation with a substantial time lag, if built at all. Recent scholarship has conceptualized this phenomenon as "cold spots/hot spots" in the worldwide web of infrastructural systems. Martin Coward, "Hot Spots/ Cold Spots: Infrastructural Politics in the Urban Age," *International Political Sociology* 9, no. 1 (2015): 96–99. This essay, however, focuses principally on the relationship between hard infrastructure and city design in the context of the United States.

5. In his majestic survey, *The Urban Millennium: The City Building Processes from the Early Middle Ages to the Present* (Carbondale: Southern Illinois University Press, 1985), Josef Konvitz notes that the sense in which we use the word *infrastructure*

today is fairly recent and "probably appeared for the first time in 1875, in French," referring to military works. For an updated view on the role of technology in the envisaged future of cities, see PCAST, "Technology and the Future of Cities," 2016, https://www.whitehouse.gov/sites/whitehouse.gov/files/images/Blog/PCAST%20 Cities%20Report%20_%20FINAL.pdf.

6. McKinsey Global Institute, *Bridging Global Infrastructure Gaps* (New York: McKinsey, 2016).

7. World Bank, *Investing in Urban Resilience* (Washington, DC: World Bank, 2015).

8. Michael Mann has described the nation-state's intrinsic desire to exercise sovereign authority (notwithstanding the form and type of government in power) by using "infrastructural power," or the state's capacity to enforce policy throughout its territory and populations via various forms of infrastructures. Michael Mann, "The Autonomous Power of the State: Its Origins, Mechanisms and Results," *European Journal of Sociology* 25, no. 2 (1984): 185–213.

9. See, for example, Ellis Armstrong, Michael Robinson, and Suellen Hoy, eds., *History of Public Works in the United States, 1776–1976* (Chicago: American Public Works Association, 1976); Nelson Manfred Blake, *Water for the Cities: A History of the Urban Water Problem in the United States* (Syracuse, NY: Syracuse University Press, 1956); and Joseph Schwieterman and Alan Mammoser, *Beyond Burnham: An Illustrated History of Planning for the Chicago Region* (Lake Forest, IL: Lake Forest College Press, 2009).

10. Michael Neuman, "Infiltrating Infrastructures: On the Nature of Networked Infrastructure," *Journal of Urban Technology* 13, no. 1 (2006): 3–31.

11. Michael Neuman, "The Long Emergence of the Infrastructure Emergency," *Town Planning Review* 85, no. 6 (2014): 795–806.

12. The predominant focus on spatial aspects and the physically fixed nature of infrastructure is perhaps best evidenced in Joel Tarr's conception of urban infrastructure as "the 'sinews' of the city." Tarr, "Evolution of Urban Infrastructure," 4. For an overview of the ongoing preoccupation with the physical dimensions of infrastructure in different parts of the world, see Mike Kerlin and Rob Palter, eds., *Voices on Infrastructure: Insights on Project Development and Finance* (New York: McKinsey, 2017); and Anupam Rastogi, *India Infrastructure Report* (New Delhi: Oxford University Press, 2006).

13. Michael Neuman and Sherri Smith, "City Planning and Infrastructure: Once and Future Partners," *Journal of Planning History* 9, no. 1 (2010): 21–42.

14. Neuman, "Infiltrating Infrastructures."

15. It is important to note here that the strict meaning of the term *public* is nowadays changing, with all types of infrastructure entailing varying degrees of private-sector involvement, even as governments continue to exercise regulatory oversight. Roads are a good example, where we seem to have gone back to the turnpike model of the nineteenth century controlled almost entirely by the private sector in different parts of the world.

16. Ibid.

17. Neuman, "Infiltrating Infrastructures."

18. Recent scholarship has, however, begun to argue that the increasing interconnected nature of infrastructure networks has created opportunities for reshaping the decision-making process, enabling new sites of experimentation and stimulating inclusive urban infrastructure. See, for instance, Aksel Ersoy, "Smart Cities as a Mechanism towards a Broader Understanding of Infrastructure Interdependencies," *Regional Science* 4, no. 1 (2017): 26–31.

19. Herbert Gans, *People and Plans: Essays on Urban Problems and Solutions* (New York: Basic Books, 1968). For a recent overview of this vein of literature, see Ralph Brand, "Urban Infrastructures and Sustainable Social Practices," *Journal of Urban Technology* 12, no. 2 (2005): 1–25. For a spirited defense, see Michael Batty and Stephen Marshal, "The Evolution of Cities: Geddes, Abercrombie, and the New Physicalism," *Town Planning Review* 80, no. 6 (2009): 551–74.

20. William Sherman, "Engaging the Field," in *Site Matters: Design Concepts, Histories and Strategies*, ed. Carol Burns and Andrea Kahn (New York: Routledge, 2005), 312.

21. Neuman, "Infiltrating Infrastructures."

22. Graham and Marvin, *When Infrastructure Fails*, 43.

23. Neuman, "Infiltrating Infrastructures," 6.

24. Robert Fishman, "1808—1908—2008: National Planning for America," Blueprint America, "PBS Reports on Infrastructure," 2010, http://www.pbs.org/wnet/blueprint america/reports/the-next-american-system/op-ed-1808-1908-2008-national-planning -for-america/?p=885,1 (emphasis in the original).

25. All by Michael Neuman, "Infiltrating Infrastructures"; "Spatial Planning Leadership by Infrastructure: An American View," *International Planning Studies* 14, no. 2 (2009): 201–17; "Infrastructure Planning for Sustainable Cities," *Geographica Helvetica* 15, no. 2 (2011): 100–107; and "Long Emergence"; Neuman and Smith, "City Planning and Infrastructure."

26. Michael Fein, *Paving the Way: New York Road Building and the American State, 1880–1956* (Lawrence: University Press of Kansas, 2008). Roads are perhaps the hardest form of infrastructure because once built, they are very difficult to relocate or realign, as evidenced in the continuing use of Roman thoroughfares and Indian trails even today.

27. Neuman and Smith, "City Planning and Infrastructure."

28. Ibid.

29. This line of approach, however, is by no means dead. Recent examples include many comprehensively conceptualized and purpose-built new towns and city extensions in different parts of the world, including those in China (for example, Ordos Kangbashi, Inner Mongolia), India (Lavasa, Maharashtra), and also in the United States (Celebration, Florida).

30. Literature describes American urban infrastructure as a blend of European ideas and adaptations and homegrown inventions and innovations. See, for instance,

R. H. Merritt, *Engineering in American Society* (Lexington: University Press of Kentucky, 1969).

31. Jon Peterson, *The Birth of City Planning in the United States* (Baltimore: Johns Hopkins University Press, 2003).

32. Neuman and Smith, "City Planning and Infrastructure."

33. Christine Boyer, *Dreaming the Rational City: The Myth of American City Planning* (Cambridge, MA: MIT Press, 1983), 67.

34. Robert Fishman, *The American Planning Tradition: Culture and Policy* (Princeton, NJ: Woodrow Wilson Centre Press, 2000).

35. Ibid.

36. Recent scholarship exploring the ongoing planetary urbanization supports this argument, finding that while "previous iterations of infrastructure were oriented toward the unitary project of the city . . . contemporary infrastructure is characterized by global reach, extending beyond the city as both place and idea. As such, the political implications of global urbanization are best read not in terms of a city-centric framework, but in terms of an infrastructural urbanism on a global scale." Coward, "Hot Spots/Cold Spots," 97. This insight, however paradoxically, raises the importance of better place-making strategies and careful design of local places.

37. Fishman, *American Planning Tradition*, 109.

38. Ibid.

39. Ibid.

40. See, for example, Hillary Ballon and Kenneth Jackson, *Robert Moses and the Modern City: The Transformation of New York* (New York: W. W. Norton, 2007).

41. Alan A. Altshuler and David E. Luberoff, *Mega-Projects: The Changing Politics of Urban Public Investment* (Washington, DC: Brookings Institution Press, 2003), 2.

42. The urban design consequences of many megaprojects, however, are not well documented. In a notable exception, Aseem Inam offers a sympathetic critique of Boston's "Big Dig," explaining how, despite the complexity of implementation and major time and cost overruns, this transit-oriented megaproject also transformed the downtown by stitching together the urban fabric (as it replaced the elevated highway), reconnected neighborhoods and the waterfront, and created new opportunities for real estate development and an impressive range of open spaces such as parks, plazas, and promenades, raising the overall quality of city life. In this respect, Inam shows how careful conception and focus on design consequences can help create better urban places even while pursuing infrastructure-centered megaprojects. Aseem Inam, *Designing Urban Transformation* (New York: Routledge, 2014).

43. Stephen Graham, *Dispersed Cities: When Infrastructure Fails* (New York: Routledge, 2010).

44. Jane Jacobs, *The Death and Life of Great American Cities* (New York: Random House, 1961).

45. Henry Cisneros, Lora Engdahl, and Kurt Schmoke, *From Despair to Hope: HOPE VI and the New Promise of Public Housing in America* (Washington, DC: Brookings Institution Press, 2009).

46. Neuman, "Spatial Planning Leadership by Infrastructure."

47. Denise Scheberle, *Federalism and Environmental Policy: Trust and the Politics of Implementation* (Washington, DC: Georgetown University Press, 2004).

48. UNEP, *UNEP Year Book, 2013* (Nairobi: UNEP, 2014).

49. Schwieterman and Mammoser, *Beyond Burnham.*

50. John M. Anderies, "Embedding Built Environments in Social-Ecological Systems: Resilience-Based Design Principles," *Building Research and Information* 42, no. 2 (2014): 130–42; Hillary Brown, *Next Generation Infrastructure: Principals for Post-industrial Public Works* (Washington, DC: Island Press, 2014).

51. Scheberle, *Federalism and Environmental Policy.*

52. Rachel Pomerance, "A Cool Hand Leads Hotlanta," *Pennsylvania Gazette* 105, no. 6 (2007): 57.

53. Margarita Angelidou, "Smart Cities Policies: A Spatial Approach," *Cities* 41, supp. 1 (2014): S3–S11; Andrew Comer and Kelly Forbes, "Urbanization in the UK: The Need for a More Focused Approach on City Infrastructure," *Civil Engineering* 169, no. 2 (2016): 53.

54. Neuman, "Infrastructure Planning for Sustainable Cities."

The City Within and the Architecture Around

Architecture of Tomorrow's City

SEAN LALLY

> The third revolution, which it seems to me we are on the verge of, is the revolution of transplantations. . . . In the future, just as the geographic world was colonized by means of transportation or communication, we will have the possibility of colonization of the human body by technology. That which favors the equipping of territories, of cities, in particular, threatens to apply to the human body, as if we had the city in the body and not the city around the body.
>
> —Paul Virilio, *The Virilio Reader*

Transportation and communication are the two revolutionary precursors that predate what Paul Virilio would characterize as the third revolution: transplantation. Advancements in these two precursors are synonymous with increased speed and collapsing of distances, as goods, people, and information travel faster. These revolutions have even extended beyond our terrestrial territory, producing an escape velocity that enabled Voyager 1, launched thirty-five years ago, to recently leave our solar system into interstellar space.

The progression of velocity and collapsing of distance are responsible for both the growth and the demise of cities, as trade routes reorganize, new methods of travel emerge (trains, planes, and automobiles), and communication technologies advance (from horses with satchels to Marconi and Wi-Fi). These advancements redefine our relationships to our territories, as distance between destinations shrinks and goods, information, and our bodies move at greater speeds. Architectural forms and typologies develop to respond to and accommodate these new methods of transportation: train stations and warehouses grew to mammoth proportions, post office centers grew in size to accommodate an increase in mail volume after paper catalogs became popular, and server centers were built with their own intricate cooling infrastructures. The rate of speed appears to continue to progress in both communication and transportation today, as corporations like Amazon and Walmart advance their shipping options from standard to two day, overnight, and same day.

Virilio's observation of this third revolution, however, places speed as a smaller player in this scenario. Cities and towns that once required static spatial interiors to accommodate services and goods are now accommodating them beyond city limits; these goods are stored in bulk until purchased through online services and delivered to your doorstep. With the human body as the site of technological "transplantation," the vehicles of communication and movement are internalized and "colonized" within. The role of architecture as a form for the body to occupy and interface with speed and available goods and services is now in question. Architecture once reflected velocity, housing goods and services that entered and exited a city. What, then, is the mandate of architectural space when vehicles of communication and service are internalized to the human body?

The arch of such a broad topic goes beyond any singular analysis, and coming to a consensus regarding what ultimately defines a city is extraordinarily difficult. Is it the presence of cultural institutions that foster the arts or the infrastructural frameworks for industry and trade? Is it the public commons of parks, plazas, and social interactions? Or is it perhaps just a point of population density? Each of these points is incomplete as an individual consideration, and the list itself could never be comprehensive. New York, Houston, and Lagos each have unique characteristics, yet each is a major urban center in the twenty-first century. The architecture of cities is a collection of the parts that are thought to define the city itself, housing those objects and information moving through a defined geographic territory. When the body becomes the epicenter of interaction (which information moves through), what becomes the role of the geographic territory, the city, and the architecture that creates the city?

THE URBANIZED BODY

The colonization of the human body by technology that monitors, reports, and—one would imagine—actuates responses, such as insulin pumps or pacemakers that help give the heart a steady rhythm, has been progressing over an extended time line. This colonization is most familiar in the form of a physical appendage, which is visible to even the most medically untrained eye as a means to correct a perceived deficiency either from birth or from a traumatic event. Appendages such as eyeglasses, hearing aids, or even a cane have moved beyond the outer envelope of our epidermis and into our bodies in the form of contact lenses, Lasik surgery, ocular implants, and titanium pins in our bones. In each of the cases mentioned above, such an action was funded, researched, and ethically cleared for action under the guise of correcting a physiological flaw or damaged sensory perception in hopes of returning function to the stasis of average (average sight, hearing, and so on). But having originated under the authority of improving health and saving lives, these solutions eventually progress technologically, ethically, and philosophically into new territories that require doctors and researchers to refrain from providing sensory perception that exceeds what is deemed average. When should an intervention halt the inevitable progression from correcting an individual's eyesight in order to bring it back to a collectively agreed-upon average to providing eyesight that is better than twenty-twenty, to go beyond the visible spectrum and into the ultraviolet or infrared? Why stop with the amplification of existing human sensory perception when we can incorporate sensory abilities of other species such as sonar and electro-magnetic navigation? Impeding on the curiosity of humanity is to go against what brought humanity to the skill sets that correct the deficiencies in the first place.

What began as an application of appendages to the human body that corrected perceived physical shortcomings has now seen massive funding research resulting in products for market consumption: devices to be worn to monitor and report vital signs in search of optimal health. Recently, Google's spin-off company Verily Life Sciences has begun mass trials to determine if its "smart devices," like watches that monitor heart rates, sleep patterns, and a range of other bodily functions, can be combined with genetic testing to improve overall health and predict future medical emergencies.[1]

As technological devices shrink in size, they can be momentarily forgotten by those individuals wearing them, even more so when they are ingested or surgically absorbed into the body. Biomaterials scientist Albert Swiston refers to one form of these devices as "ingestibles." They move through the digestive system and are capable of providing information about the health of soldiers or astronauts that experience extreme environmental conditions or trauma patients without having to make contact with the skin.[2] With successful implantation, the user is rarely reminded of their existence; as these devices colonize the human body from within, those individuals casually observ-ing the body from the outside would fail to even recognize their presence. And though the distinction between appendage and internalization is worth further discussion, it is the approach to health that is of critical importance here.

An increased bandwidth of sensory perception not only amplifies and extends the range of information available for making decisions about the surrounding environments but also affects the materials architects can manipulate and design with that those enhanced senses can perceive. What I would like to highlight here is a shift in medical care from repair and optimization of body function to a state of continual monitoring and reporting. The monitoring of the body's physiological state (and one would assume eventually its physiological and emotional state) provides architects with a source of reliable information, one that hasn't existed prior to today's collection of large data groups. As we'll see, this perpetual feedback loop transcends the body and includes the incorporation of the context itself that the body moves within. A communication and dialogue between the body and the context it is situated within also serve to collapse the distinction between the two.

From Vitruvius to Leonardo da Vinci's representation of the Vitruvian Man and well beyond, architects have worked with metrics to quantify and synthesize knowledge that can be represented to inform the shaping of material form to define spaces for that body to occupy. Increased knowledge about how the body perceives and responds to color, temperature, and sound has been reflected in the spaces that the architectural discipline has sought to advance.

If biological and technological advancements before were applied to the human body to repair deficiencies and injury, one could say this offered the possibility of a more shared spatial experience. As the body is often judged on criteria of accepted norms—sensory perceptions related to sight, hearing, or mobility—each requires a manipulation of either body or site to make a public space capable of being experienced and shared equally. The repair associated with increased medical knowledge and technology offers the opportunity for spatial environments to be experienced by all and offer shared public space. When this is not possible, then physical space is manipulated to meet standards of accessibility (ADA [Americans with Disabilities Act] accessibility). As individuals choose to exceed our sensorial averages through wearables and bioengineering, shared space has the potential to fragment.

The continuous monitoring and reporting of the colonized bodies and their environmental contexts only serve to intensify that fragmentation, as individuals choose from a commercially available spectrum of urbanized body. Unlike the repair or correction of an individual's trauma or deficiency that has near consensus for moral good, the colonization or urbanization of the body as it relates to monitoring and reporting will likely play out altogether differently, with some choosing to engage this internal urbanization on a sliding gradient of integration. This will occur based on a range of criteria, such as socioeconomic situation, religion, and community engagement.

When information resources are increasingly accessible to the body, the city is no longer solely around the body as physical context but also in the body; then we're discussing the urbanization of the body. What specifically does it mean to have an urbanized body, and can we think of bodies—either as singular states chosen by individuals or phased over a duration of time—as urban, suburban, and rural? Designing to meet a perceived bodily average (according to proportion, ergonomics, and sensory perception) will shift to acknowledging a spectrum of bodily function; the urban, suburban, and rural bodies will move among each other at all times.

As the body absorbs communication directly from additional bodies without the need for a physically defined space to mediate that activity (cell phones versus phone booths), and that same body can be monitored and responded to by its environmental context (traffic on roads is monitored by the movement of cell phones on highways, and lights in offices are turned on remotely by fob key sensors we carry with us), then it can be said that our bodies are in a dialogue with their spatial context.

Our handheld devices, wristwatches in direct contact with our bodies, and medical devices that sit below the surface of our skin belong to a growing list of devices embedded with sensors that reinforce a dialogue between objects and bodies. Often referred to as the "Internet of things," these devices—everything from baby monitors and coffee machines to running shoes and ingestible medical devices—not only track and sense the variables requested but also communicate with each other: your coffee maker with your toaster, your phone with your baby monitor, and your surgically installed insulin pump with your doctor.

Precision is not a novel concept in architecture. Precision is demanded in many variations: the translation of architectural intentions and representation into material form as well as the demands and expectations of those that finance the work or regulations (codes and zoning) that demand compliance. Precision is expected in operation as well. This includes energy consumption, organizational flexibility, and the expected behavior of individuals using the space. Some requirements appear more like expectations, while others are articulated deliverables. Expectations that can be represented and articulated with drawings and calculations (dimensions, material choices, and cost) are seen as "articulated deliverables" to be executed and judged for success or failure. Expectations, as they pertain to user behavior, are often seen as being on the periphery of architectural control. This form of precision is intentional and goal oriented but difficult to guarantee and deliver.

The colonization of the body, or, more precisely, the colonization as it pertains to health monitoring and reporting, opens the potential for collecting metrics related to bodies' physiological responses that can inform environmental decision making. Even the entry-level watches today are capable of monitoring and recording an individual's heart rate, information that can be extrapolated to determine the wearer's response to specific designed spaces or interactions with environments. Such a fundamental data set provides information about an individual's response beyond that of the watch's initially specified goal of monitoring health and exercise. Couple this information with current GPS technologies, and user location can continually be monitored to determine an individual's choice of path of travel or time spent in particular locations. This precision related to monitoring and reporting of the body is often perceived as subjective and experiential. Subjective experiences of the body in spaces are increasingly capable of being quantified and therefore appropriated by the architect for design decisions.

As the body is increasingly urbanized, internalizing access to information and services related to communication, health, and commerce, the built environment that the body moves through is required to take on new responsibilities and shapes. In other words, opportunities are available for architects to reimagine not only the architectural form that the human body moves within and around but also the fundamental dialogue between architectural shapes and the human body's engagement with those shapes. Both are open for design, and the two are capable of being tuned to one another like never before.

TUNING

Density is a measurement of accumulation in regards to our cities, going beyond the physical mass of buildings. It can also measure information and resources. The usefulness of that density is related to the proximity of the human body to the accumulation. In terms of environments, this is broadly categorized as urban, suburban, or rural. In this example, density is geographically static, and it is the body that transitions between, in, and around. But when density of information and the accumulation of resources are transferred to the body, what are the implications to the geographic locales and the architectural shapes that define them?

When both the human body and the environment it is located within are engaged (the first through a colonization of technologies and the second a willful manipulation of both local microclimates and global climates), a negotiation occurs that implies a degree of impact on both. When this is done intentionally through design, it could be said that the two are tuned to one another. In such an approach, architecture would not be seen as a third party, built to mediate between the body and its environmental context; instead, architectural design would be the design of a context where the two parties (body and environment) would be more actively tuned to one another.

Street lighting is clear example of such a tuning. The light emitted from the overhead lighting structure along streets or park walkways does not replicate the energy spectrums of the sun. Instead, this light we see is specifically produced to respond to the spectrum of visible light our human eyes can perceive. This wavelength is roughly 400–700 nanometers. Anything smaller than 400 nanometers, and the wavelength reaches into the ultraviolet range; if more than 700, the wavelength is in the ultraviolet. Both are beyond the wavelength spectrum that our eyes can perceive. You could therefore state that street lighting is tuned specifically to the human body. In this specific example, the tuning is one way, that is, the material is tuned to the body; the two are not simultaneously open for manipulation. The second important point to be made about street lighting is that it is often dismissed as infrastructural or simply as a utilitarian safety requirement, when in fact it would be more accurate to characterize street lighting as architectural. After all, street lighting has all the hallmarks of architecture. It has a discernible form produced by the light, it has an interior, and it provides resources for activities against the darkness of night.

As the body continues to absorb or colonize resources of communication and information, the static artifacts of architectural forms (and the resources nested within those forms) are no longer moored in place. They instead follow the body as it moves, and the environmental locales that the body locates for itself are free for experimentation and new actions.

The architectural act of tuning the body and the environment through technological colonization of the body and environmental manipulation is an action on two subjects (body and environment). Through the lens of the architectural discipline, this can be seen as a design decision. This, however, is not unique. Evolution is a tuning of a species to its context, though in most cases the two are not acted upon simultaneously. It is an evolutionary progression responsible for the human body as it stands prior to technological colonization.

Alexander von Humbolt in his 1807 book *On the Geography of Plants* is seen as the first to make the correlation between plant species and the surrounding context of climate, latitude, altitude, soil, geology, and so forth. This is seen as a precursor to what is referred to now as environments.[3] Von Humbolt identified the importance of the environmental variables that inform plant species and are responsible for plant species' variation (leaf size, width, and the like) in geographic locales with variable differences.

In regards to the human body, Sanford Kwinter looks to the nervous system as a site of social, political, and psychedelic innovation, as he places the brain against the "larger backdrop of environmental history." Kwinter characterizes this as neuroecology, saying sensory input is not immaterial; it is the environment itself, and it is the "becoming brain."[4] Kwinter states that the development of the human brain and nervous system is as much a response to the predatory species and populations hunting and placing pressure on humans as it is to the climatic variables that the human body experienced. Humans, both in body and in mind, grew to respond to the actions and traits of multiple predatory species as well as to their climatic context. As Kwinter reminds us, we as humans are not *within* nature and the environment; we are the environment.

The processes of our brains and the sensory responses of our nervous systems can be seen as continually evolving, as it is clear we defer to artificial processing powers and external data-storage devices. Computers process calculations faster than our minds are capable of doing, and we store our memories in photographs, writings, and videos on external storage devices capable of being recalled when needed. A colonized body simply ties those calculations and storage more directly to the physical body.

Increased speed and storage are but two examples of extending existing human processes. Our cities today respond to and make decisions that inform our behaviors: the timing of traffic lights and streetlights appears as a simple action we seldom question. Advancements in artificial intelligence do more than move cars, integrating them into an Internet of things that includes network appliances, vehicles, buildings, and cameras that together are able to process ever-larger data sets. Is it uncomfortable to realize the colonized bodies are potentially part of that increasing data set connected to the Internet of things?

Kwinter's neuroecology illustrates the nervous system's evolution in response to both climatic variables as well as the behavior of species in a shared environment. Humans today are responsible for the evolution on the two sides, both the enhanced brainpower and the behaviors of the environment we locate ourselves within. The pursuit of an absolute control of global environments is in no way the intended focus here, but the distinction between the two could be difficult to discern at times. However, it could also be seen as negligent for the discipline, as well as lost opportunity, for having a voice of leadership in a topic so heavily tied to climate change, affecting an overwhelming percentage of humanity.

Our options for responding to this crisis are not limited to a single action or disciplinary approach. This isn't purely a technological or political problem to be fixed. Architecture has a role to play, and it is potentially much more critical than is often assumed—not only in delivering responsible construction but also in shaping the discourse and possibly even reframing the problem itself.

Humanity has shaped this planet. It has changed the chemical composition of the atmosphere, and it has eradicated plant, animal, and insect species. It has also had a geologic influence, as we mine to remove hydrocarbons that fuel our civilizations and then replace them with our own form of geology (known as concrete) that has become so prevalent in construction that more than half of all the concrete ever used was produced in the past twenty years.[5] Let's not forget the fact that our global communication revolution, which has produced a veil of satellites and space debris, is orbiting the outer edges of our planet.

But the manipulation of the planet goes beyond examples of eradication and pollution of both known and unmapped territories. It also includes the introduction of new synthetic and hybridized species of plants, animals, and insects as well as assemblages of metals, silicon, and software that have sparked debate about artificial intelligence and the potential spark of a new consciousness.

There's no shortage of discourse in regards to the influence humans have had on shaping Earth. A new term, *Anthropocene*, is probably the most succinct way to describe this current epoch we find ourselves not only belonging to but responsible for creating. As Kwinter reminds us, we as humans are not distinct from the "nature we are located *within* and should instead be seen as *being* that 'nature.'"

The urbanized body can at once reinforce the argument that the body is distinct from its environmental context, as it is populated with technologies that can quickly be pointed to as artificial and man-made. A populated urban environment that seems to reciprocate in integration of such technologies would, however, serve only to highlight shared similarities of the body and the environment. The progression forward would appear to some to be a technological question, one that requires a better understanding of human biology, environmental science, computer science, and artificial intelligence, to name just a few relevant fields. Technology alone would lead to some glaring omissions that any architect, landscape architect, or planner would quickly point out. The distinction I would like to make here, however, is that the broader architectural and planning discipline can best influence this progression not only in serving to implement advancements but also in shaping the call for them in the first place. This is a distinction that Arnulf Grubler, who studies the major transitions of energy and technology, would characterize as pulling versus pushing our futures.

PULLING AHEAD

Historically speaking, energy transitions (wood to coal, coal to oil, oil to renewables) take decades, if not centuries, to occur. This is the focus of the work of Arnulf Grubler as he traces the technological and societal developments related to these transitions. More specifically, he makes the distinction between attempts to push these transitions as opposed to pulling them.[6]

Pushing occurs through regulation, policy, and mandates by governing agencies. This differs from pulling, which doesn't negate these agencies but is much more closely related to services or visions that entice consumers, users, or the public to engage. These modes of pulling and pushing may be identified through the work of Grubler as they pertain to energy and technological transitions, but they are also analogous to the architectural profession.

Providing visions of alternate futures is something that architecture has been rather good at in the past. There are many examples of thoughtful models of potential futures that play out current trends in technology, politics, and sociology in an attempt to skew those trends into a specific and often plausible option. A good example of this mode of approach would be architect Cedric Price and his Fun Palace project, which he initiated with Joan Littlewood. This was a project without a client or even a site in the beginning. He would go on to intertwine a wide range of contemporary discourse and theories, including cybernetics, information theory, and even theater into a socially interactive public space.[7] He collaborated with people such as cyberneticians Gordon Pask and Norbert Wiener. And though the project was never built, it had immense influence. You could say it acted as a form of inspiration and set the groundwork for many architects' future work. No doubt, it even informed the research of his collaborators. This is because it was more than a design exercise that saw its way into a few architecture publications; it was a project that was in development for close to a decade and not only included a large, diverse collaborative team but also engaged politicians, developers, and financiers. The Fun Palace pulled our profession forward and did the same for anyone who took the time to understand its social objectives. Norman Bel Geddes's vision for the General Motors Pavilion at the 1939 World's Fair did the same for our collective imagination, as did dozens of projects by Archigram. The value of these projects exists in being able to influence expectations.

This is particularly important today, as we face a plethora of uncertainties, from the climatic changes of our planet to the biology of our human bodies, as well as questions about how technologies such as artificial intelligence and augmented reality will mediate between the two (our planet and our bodies). As Stanislaw Lem said, "There are no answers, only choices." And unfortunately, most conversations related to these topics revolve around the belief that our problems have answers. These are massive issues that need to be addressed on multiple fronts. Technological solutions are only one of those fronts. Focusing on these problems solely through the lens of a search for a technological solution gives the impression that we have a problem that can be fixed. And when a problem is believed to be fixable, it is assumed that the solution gives us something that looks like it did prior to the problem. This is a very important conversation to have, because as long as people see our environmental situation as a problem that can be fixed, they will always carry in their minds images of a past that they believe we can return to. What would be better would be to provide alternative imagery of a future that is both optimistic and able to carry with it the potential for change. These images and scenarios (not intending to be predictive but instead plausible) would work to stretch the imagination and prepare us for what alternate lifestyles could be.

The urbanized body and the role of architectural shapes that engage that body are at the center of this discussion. That same intentional manipulation and colonization of the body has already been playing itself out on a global scale of our environments. The geographic locales we define as urban centers have always engaged their environmental contexts, both internally, referring to the context within specified borders, the parks, and public spaces, and externally, directly beyond those borders. The role of parks, shared public spaces, and commons has the potential to become increasingly critical for cities that require flexibility and open dialogue with diverse human bodies of varying "density."

The architect is in the position to play a substantial role in pulling a very complex and multifaceted discussion forward, one that integrates technol-

ogy, ethics, and policy, as well as how and where these exchanges will occur between the body and the environment. The site of this engagement is
therefore of critical importance, not only in the activities and programs on
that site but also in its ability to place at the foreground the messiness associated with privacy and ethics of technologies and public use. It's only by
engaging a conversation with the public about appropriate uses of an array
of topics intersected here (individual data, artificial intelligence, energy uses,
climate change) that progress can be made. Without this transparency, public
confidence will be eroded. Therefore, this work belongs in our urban public
spaces, not in private buildings.

A 2014 poll commissioned by the Royal Statistical Society found that "32%
of respondents had low levels of trust in Internet companies in general but
54% had low trust in them to use personal data appropriately." There are likely
several reasons for such polling. One is clearly the existence of examples that
demonstrate such mishandling of personal data, including the recent ruling
by the UK Information Commissioner's Office against the operator of three
London hospitals for breaking civil law when it gave health data to Google's
London-based subsidiary DeepMind. DeepMind was seeking to develop a
software application that could check for signs of acute kidney injuries.[8] And
this isn't an isolated event. Any consumer who wears a watch or wristband to
track their health or sleeping habits must question what is to become of that
data. In particular, if that company were to fail, such data would make for a
wonderful golden parachute, packaged and sold to competitors to reimburse
early investors. The second reason for such polling results must in some way
be attributed to the omission of public conversation. This is in part due to
a lack of transparency by the corporations developing the technologies but
also due to a lack of accountability by the users. The current prevalence of
technology in user lifestyles makes it difficult to identify a site for evaluation.
Exercise, health care, business, and social media are each intertwined within
our daily activities, making it difficult to recuse ourselves when competitiveness, health, and safety are advertised to demand their use.

To best nurture debate and dialogue, a defined public architectural territory
is best suited to push experimentation while maintaining transparency. Public
parks (or at least a subset of them) are best suited for this. The public park
has an origin in the English commons, which represented a combination of
natural and cultural resources accessible to all within society. Though both
definitions of natural and cultural resources continue to evolve, the physical
locale of the public commons, or park, still carries within it the potential to
synthesize debate and common good. Defining a territorial locale simultaneously demarcates where actions are occurring (which can otherwise be

very difficult to know) while opening the throttle for more ambitious experimentation and revisions. Most important for the architectural discipline, it provides a site to give shape to and exercise our expertise in aesthetics and spatial organization.

Without determining the specifics for any particular design, key attributes can be extrapolated that can help outline opportunities and potential limitations. It is important to remember in discourse of this nature that architects were not responsible for the technological development of concrete, iron, steel, glass, or plastics; however, it was architecture that reappropriated these technological advancements, exploiting their unique proclivities to produce novel spaces and shapes that coincided with cultural pressures of their day. In many respects, this current trajectory is no different from previous epochs of disciplinary action. The variables associated with aesthetics, spatial organization, and social pressures might be unique to today, though the disciplinary procedures of architecture remain rather constant. This is to say, architecture has managed to demonstrate in the past an ability to synthesize disparate technological advancements in materials and productions with current social pressures in order to produce unique physical forms and spaces that become emblematic of the times. This is probably most clearly demonstrated in the late nineteenth century by the Crystal Place or perhaps the Grand Palais des Champs-Élysées. These are architectural projects that synthesized the national pride of two countries that wanted to display not only the mass production of domestic products but also the vegetative collections from their global colonies that required new artificial interior spaces, made possible from new smelting techniques of iron and larger plates of glass. Architecture can make the case that it is in the best position to synthesize and test these current technological and social pressures.

What, then, might architects look toward, specifically today as we address aesthetic and spatial implications of an urbanized body and manipulated climate?

Malleable Space

There is a clear lineage within architecture interested in movable, flexible space. This can be seen in kinetic structures that physically move to change their shape or large open-plan structures in which interior wall partitions can be easily installed and removed as flexibility demands (Mies van der Rohe's National Gallery in Berlin). As the earlier street-lighting example demonstrates, energy systems on the exterior quickly experience entropy, dissipating into their surroundings. This is usually seen as a limitation, but that same streetlight is easily manipulated in its color and intensity and is able to be turned on or off or made stronger or weaker when needed. This simple example of street lighting can be carried further with sound, temperature, and electromagnetic fields. Malleability of space translates to flexibility for creating and removing material presence, and this is a quality that is unique to this future architecture.

Updatable Materials

When such a large percentage of the architecture's shape comes from the energy released to produce exterior microclimates and sensorial receptors receiving information from the human body, it is the small technological devices, such as the lightbulb or wearable, in the architectural system that can be easily updated. As technological solutions advance in relation to efficiencies and the performance of these devices, they become more easily updatable. A shift from high-pressure sodium street lighting to LED is an example in which it is the lightbulb alone that is updatable. Tesla vehicles regularly receive software updates that "add new features and functionality" to their cars.[9] These include improved autopilot controls as well as improved battery life. Architectural forms constructed from stone, steel, and glass can appear static not only in shape but also in their ability to keep pace with technological advancements.

Evolving Social Experience

Many of the emerging trends from this discourse are simply previous discriminatory practices revisited. When it comes to public parks and spaces in cities, two of the last hurdles to democratize public spaces are seen to be access to public transportation and the ADA. Both are seen as critical in making public space accessible to all. In these examples, the same public space is technically accessible to all, but as some of us may have experienced while riding a city train that plunges belowground, not everyone maintains their network provider and therefore access to the Internet or communication. Much like two individuals might today have different access to Internet connection based on separate cellular providers and equipment, individual access and ability to perceive sensory information will vary along socioeconomic status, technological demographics, and health, making the same public space unique among multiple user groups.

Ethical and Moral Dilemmas

Ethical and moral issues inevitably arise when there is willful manipulation of global climate and human physiology. It is through these first spatial scenarios that potential outcomes can most completely be explored.

New Conversations about Environmental Change

This work seeks to give energy a public face that excites and inspires a progressive discussion about our inevitably changing environments and the role architecture can play.

CONCLUSION

The colonization of the body that Virilio describes sets a tone of reluctant observation and weariness to what appears to be an inevitable evolution of human experience. The engineering and commercialization of technologies initially appear to be the main orchestrators of our future, leaving the rest of us to be on alert and skeptical of this ongoing evolution. I hope that this discussion illustrates that there is a potential for meaningful dialogue and direction of this evolution and that it is best served by the architectural discipline. The role of the architect is not to directly develop alternate technologies, pass legislation, or to hold corporations accountable to ethics violations, but instead to orchestrate spatial and territorial sites in which these issues can be foreshadowed and demonstrated. By amplifying and engaging this discourse through the core strengths of the architectural discipline—defining material boundaries, organizing spatial relationships, and exploring new shape aesthetics, all while placing user experience at the center of the conversation—architecture can fold in and act as an epicenter for much broader dialogue and experimentation.

Incorporating growing pressures in technology and evolving understandings of nature and the human body are not new tasks for the architectural discipline. However, the speed of that development and implementation, as well as the scale of the potential ramifications, could be argued as a unique period in time.

The biological and chemical recipe that we've come to think we know here on Earth is of course not consistent across the vast spectrum of environments across the planet's surface, or even below it. With a history of more than four billion years, our current history can also only ever be seen as a snapshot in time. Increasing our bandwidth of imagination and acceptance of what a responsible, healthy future looks like here on our planet will require something more than technological solutions to fix a problem; it will require a set of elastic expectations, nurtured by imagery and social scenarios in regards to what the twenty-first century will bring.

The current cultural image, for lack of a better word, of a healthy Earth and what that looks like is simplistic and quite frankly stunted. This is because the image that many people carry along with them of what a responsible future for Earth looks like is based on what they assume it looked like in the recent past. This is understandable to some extent, assuming you can point to a period in time in our past in which that ideal environment and current collection of global cultural achievements coexisted (instant global communication, billions of humans, a food supply to feed them all, to name a few). Our current cultural achievements and the resulting global environment are difficult to untangle from each other at this point.

The relationship between the human body and the global environment is a continuous dialogue. It should not be seen as resolvable or capable of reaching an ideal final state. Just as no architecture is capable of characterizing anything more than the pressures and opportunities of its day, it is important to remember that the current dialogue of environment and body is elastic and will likely never reach a point of consensus or equilibrium. Architectural design is therefore a necessary medium and site to continue to nurture that discourse and conversation.

Notes

1. Hetan Shah, "The DeepMind Debacle Demands Dialogue on Data," *Nature* 547, no. 259 (2017), https://www.nature.com/news/the-deepmind-debacle-demands-dialogue -on-data-1.22330.

2. Rae Ellen Bichell, "A Tiny Pill Monitors Vital Signs from Deep Inside the Body," http://www.npr.org/sections/health-shots/2015/11/18/455953304/a-tiny-pill-monitors -vital-signs-from-deep-inside-the-body.

3. Sanford Kwinter, "'Neuroecology: Noted toward a Synthesis," in *The Psychopathologies of Cognitive Capitalism, Part 2* (Berlin: Archive Books, 2017), 328.

4. Ibid.

5. Adam Vaughan, "Human Impact Has Pushed Earth into the Anthropocene, Scientists Say," *Guardian*, https://www.theguardian.com/environment/2016/jan/07/ human-impact-has-pushed-earth-into-the-anthropocene-scientists-say.

6. Oliver Morton, *The Planet Remade, How Geoengineering Could Change the World* (Princeton, NJ: Princeton University Press, 2016), 195.

7. Stanley Mathews, "'The Fun Palace: Cedric Price's Experiment in Architecture and Technology," *Technoetic Arts: A Journal of Speculative Research* 3, no. 2 (2005): 81.

8. Shah, "DeepMind Debacle."

9. Tesla, "Support," https://www.tesla.com/support/software-updates.

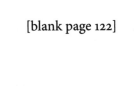
[blank page 122]

PART THREE
SYNTHESIS

[blank page 124]

The Power to Move People

Public Art and Public Transit

BILL BURTON

Public infrastructure: everybody loves it. Business and labor, elected officials and agency honchos, architects and planners, taxpayers and citizens—all of them recognize that at any scale, public assets foster economic growth, build community, establish local identity, and improve residents' quality of life. Both the construction projects and the completed works provide a multitude of job opportunities.

No, wait—everybody hates public infrastructure. The edifices are often prematurely obsolete. The projects are impossible to plan or to budget over the lengthy time spans of construction, operation, and maintenance. Their massive expense burdens taxpayers and drains funds from needed human services. The structures form barriers that divide neighborhoods, the planning process excludes and ignores whole segments of the community, and the economic benefits accrue only to developers, landlords, and home owners who can afford to live in gentrifying neighborhoods, while longtime residents are economically displaced. Job creation is temporary and inequitable.

The 2017 Urban Forum brought together people from all of the aforementioned stakeholder and interest groups, along with their academic counterparts, to talk through this complex love-hate relationship with the public infrastructure of work and play. On behalf of the cochairs, Cook County Board president Toni Preckwinkle and University of Illinois at Chicago chancellor Michael Amiridis, program director Michael Pagano welcomed discussants and attendees to the twenty-third annual UIC-hosted conference on the urban challenges of contemporary society.

Pagano, who is dean of the UIC College of Urban Planning and Public Affairs, noted that the political ground had shifted dramatically and unexpectedly since the theme and subtopics of the 2017 Urban Forum were finalized the year before. At that time, 2016's presidential contenders were in surprisingly close agreement on the need for an infrastructure overhaul on a national scale. During the campaign, perhaps the only fact not in dispute between Donald Trump and Hillary Clinton was the dilapidated state of the nation's transportation infrastructure—the physical networks that foster commerce and mobility. Most of these structures, built before 1960, were and are in a state of crumbling disrepair, and $3.6 trillion in public investment would be needed by 2020 to upgrade them, according to the American Society of Civil Engineers.

An economic—and political—side benefit of such expenditure is the huge number of jobs it would create. The Council of Economic Advisers' most recent estimate, from 2011, is that every billion dollars in federal highway and transit investment supports thirteen thousand jobs for one year. Clinton, the odds-on favorite, had called for a five-year $275 billion package of infrastructure spending. Candidate Trump, in response, said he would "at least double" what Clinton planned to spend. Then an election happened. In June 2017, President Trump called for an infrastructure rebuilding plan that would use $200 billion in federal funding aimed at leveraging a total investment of $1 trillion. But by the time of the Urban Forum in September, the president and Republican-majority lawmakers had spent the first eight months of the new administration enmeshed in repeated and unsuccessful attempts to repeal the 2009 Affordable Care Act and had just begun to shift their focus to budget and tax cutting. An infrastructure bill was not on the horizon.

Ignoring a crisis does not solve it, of course, and just as infrastructure planning, design, and construction proceed with or without an infusion of federal aid, so too the Urban Forum forged ahead with vision and optimism about how projects can be conceived and executed in the public interest—and how community input can and should help steer the process.

The very term *infrastructure* would have been unfamiliar to most people just thirty years ago, Pagano noted, but more recently has come into the American lexicon to represent the roads, bridges, and water and sewer systems that cities and states invest in to promote economic growth and development. Such physical assets, he said, are the ones that come to mind when one thinks of the return on investment of infrastructure, as they enhance the economic profile of a community or state. But parks and green space are also fixed-asset public investments, sometimes equally long-lived, that are not intended so much to promote economic growth and development as to "shape the feel of the city, to improve or enhance the quality-of-life, and to make the kind of society that we want to have." Even these quality-of-life public assets can be freighted with controversy, as reflected in fresh conflicts over Confederate Civil War monuments and in the never-ending constitutional debates over religious symbols in public spaces.

Pagano went on to clarify, for the purposes of the conference, the nomenclature of "hard" versus "soft" infrastructure. Rather than separating architectural assets from human, institutional, educational, and cultural resources—or dividing built physical structures from open public land—the definitions would be based on their referents' primary socioeconomic purpose. Hard infrastructure would be any public asset intended to boost economic development, while soft infrastructure would be those elements intended to improve residents' quality of life. Over the course of the day's conversations, this shorthand would prove useful, although the line dividing the two was often shown to be blurry or nonexistent.

To begin the day's program, Carol Ross Barney, an award-winning architect whose forty-year career has focused on projects in the public realm, opened with a review of recent works completed by her self-named design firm that are familiar to Chicago residents and visitors: the revamp of the Chicago Transit Authority (CTA)'s Cermak-McCormick Place and Morgan Street elevated train stations and the Chicago Riverwalk. Her aim was to demonstrate the power that design can have on infrastructure, and she chose to focus on three "smaller, grittier" projects that embrace principles of access and equity along with beauty and identity—and that took shape within budget, space, and bureaucratic constraints. Together, the projects she described encompassed work and play as well as soft and hard infrastructure by any definition.

The two CTA train stations "transformed their neighborhoods," Ross Barney said—although in the case of Morgan Street, the transformation may have come first. Both the transportation and the architecture writers at the *Chicago Tribune*, while lauding the design, argued that the station followed rather than fostered the resurgence of the trendy West Loop. Morgan, one of the original 1893 stations of the Lake Street "L," had been razed in 1949, when the CTA determined it was no longer needed in the "fallow ring," as Ross Barney called it, between the Loop and Chicago's new suburbs. The new "infill" station, serving the CTA's Green Line and Pink Line, was created in response to a long lobbying campaign by West Loop merchants and residents and is already serving 150 percent of its projected ridership since it opened in 2012.

Designing an infill station is challenging due to limited space when cost considerations require the use of existing track. At Morgan the designers solved the site limitations by appropriating small paved spaces on either side of the street for fare collection and extending the footprint upward, thus also creating a visible icon, directing attention to the CTA stop. At the Green Line's Cermak-McCormick Place station—also an infill, replacing an 1890s stop that had been demolished in 1978—similar site constraints imposed a center platform only fourteen feet wide between the existing tracks. The designers' solution was a canopy that spans both tracks without the need for columns on the platform, creating the signature steel tube that encloses the station and serves as a windbreak. The wheelchair-accessible Cermak station filled a 2.5-mile gap in CTA rapid-transit service, and Ross Barney said more than twenty-three hundred hotel rooms and thirty-five hundred apartments have been announced in the area served by the station, along with the ten-thousand-seat DePaul Arena.

An even more impactful redevelopment of an existing asset was the third example project Ross Barney presented, the Chicago Riverwalk. The vision for a riverwalk was not a new one, having been a part of Daniel Burnham and Edward Bennett's 1909 *Plan of Chicago*, as rendered by American artist Jules Guérin. These views included a promenade around the large turning basin at the confluence where the Main and North Branches of the river empty into the South Branch. But later, when bridge houses were built, those structures had to sit right in the water, blocking passage on the riverbanks. A walk along the river forced pedestrians to climb twenty-two feet of stairs at every bridge, cross four lanes of traffic, and descend again on the other side of the street.

The Riverwalk project was made feasible by the renovation of the seventy-six-year-old two-tiered Wacker Drive, begun in 2002. The city created a TIF (tax-increment financing) district to pay for the renewal, and planning of the Riverwalk began. The first hurdle was a legislative one. Because waterways are under federal control, the course of a river or location of a riverbank cannot be altered without congressional action. "We couldn't build new land, and we couldn't build around" the bridge houses, Ross Barney explained, so the city had to go to Congress and the U.S. Department of Transportation to obtain rights to build new land into the river—twenty feet wide under each bridge and twenty-five feet wide between bridges.

The designers' concept for the Riverwalk was to create a continuous walkway but use the bridges to define individual "rooms" with their own unique identity and landscape. The project proceeded in phases, moving downstream westward along the backward-flowing main stem. The first section, opened in

2015, stretches three blocks. One room includes docks for yachts and pleasure boats; another is a landing spot for human-powered vessels. The third room is a river theater, where the designers sought to "turn the river up to the city, and the city down to the river," with a monumental staircase that also functions as an accessible entrance to the Riverwalk. In 2016 three more blocks opened, including one with a zero-depth water feature and another with floating gardens that provide a habitat for fish on their underside. Lack of suitable habitat has become the limiting factor for fish and wildlife populations since water quality improved after treatment standards were upgraded in 2011.

The city's next project is to extend the Riverwalk along the South Branch, from Lake Street to Ping Tom Park in Chinatown. At the Civic Opera House, built in the 1920s when the river was at its worst, the building's west wall drops straight down to the river, so additional federal permits to alter the riverbank are needed. Farther downstream, various developments are under way, and the city now has an ordinance that requires any new or substantially remodeled property to provide thirty feet of publicly accessible right-of-way for the Riverwalk.

The Riverwalk is an asset for Chicagoans and visitors alike, Ross Barney said, already enabling people to walk from Lake Street all the way to the museum campus without having to cross traffic. Buildings completed since the inception of the Riverwalk total over $2 billion in value, with more than one thousand rental units and 2.3 million square feet of office space. The project, she noted, was built without Chicago tax dollars, under a loan from the Department of Transportation that the city services with usage fees. Perhaps most important, she said, projects like the Riverwalk have an impact throughout the city, because they "not only change the quality of life; they change what people believe they can do with their environment."

The Urban Forum's two panel discussions would later explore at length the equity issues and need for community input in infrastructure planning, but Ross Barney touched on these concerns as well. With the success of the Riverwalk, Mayor Rahm Emanuel asked the Metropolitan Planning Council, an independent nonprofit, to study the river for further improvements possible in the next several decades. Ross Barney's firm is supporting that study by conducting community meetings and surveying Chicagoans about their relationship with the river and its 150 miles of riverbank. "The river goes everywhere in the city. It doesn't discriminate. It doesn't care about economics or race," she said, and she offered examples of public input in two communities.

At Goose Island, on the city's gentrifying North Side, officials had considered filling in the narrow east channel. But after soliciting community opinion that favored playing up the natural aspects of the river, the designers proposed a floating wetlands park similar to the one created downtown along the Main Branch. In Pilsen and Little Village, two adjacent predominantly Latino communities just southwest of the Loop, a series of blind canals were dug long ago to serve as docks for factories that have since been abandoned. In response to community concerns, the Metropolitan Water Reclamation District began pumping the water to remediate the fetid, stagnant canals. Nearby, the Chicago Park District created the 21.5-acre La Villita Park on a reclaimed brownfield and former Environmental Protection Agency Superfund site. Further investment will be needed to turn the canal area into usable land, she said, but if water quality continues to improve, the long-term vision is for a swimming area in the Chicago River at Little Village.

In response to an audience question about equity in public transit, Ross Barney acknowledged that the rebuilt CTA stations she discussed, by virtue of their locations, do primarily serve riders who are upper middle class. Equity issues, she agreed, are particularly acute in regards to transit. "That's *the* question for the future of our city," she said. In contrast to the river, the CTA clearly does not extend to all Chicago communities. Leanne Redden of the Regional Transportation Authority (RTA) confirmed later in the day that plans to extend the Red Line on the South Side from 95th to 135th Street were on hold due to a lack of funding. To help address questions of equity, Ross Barney said her firm is making a data map with overlays for transportation, education, and average household income to identify advantageous and equitable transportation corridors, and the city has similar data projects under way. In the same vein, she said that as part of the Riverwalk/Great Rivers project, the Metropolitan Planning Council is helping administer a fund from the Chicago Community Trust to distribute planning money to affected communities.

BUILDING A JUST CITY:
SHAPING COMMUNITIES' QUALITY OF LIFE

Green areas are essential to the health of an urban area, Ross Barney said, and following her talk the morning's first panel convened to discuss how to meet this need for residents in neighborhoods throughout the city. How can community interests best be incorporated in planning for parks and playgrounds, public art, and architectural design during a time of scant resources and ample social and political distrust? WBEZ's Alexandra Salomon sat down with urban planner Gia Biagi, principal at Studio Gang; Scott Stewart, executive director of the Millennium Park Foundation; Juanita Irizarry, executive director of Friends of the Parks; and artist and educator Miguel Aguilar. The discussion was not so much a how-to seminar, as the distinguished panel had to confront stubborn dilemmas from the artistic to the financial and organizational. The visions of artists and architects, city officials and private philanthropists, and community members and tourists can often be in conflict with one another, starting with design and continuing through programming.

Salomon began by noting that surveys since the 2016 election indicate that barely half of Americans have faith in their democracy and only one in three say they trust each other. If such national statistics are relevant to the visible social and cultural divides in a city like Chicago, can we design and create parks and public art that enable and encourage people to engage with each other?

Design does direct the human interactions that occur in public spaces, Biagi said, and is a focus of her work as an urban planner at an architecture firm, much as it was in her previous positions as a city and park district official. She noted a strange finding of a Knight Foundation study from a decade ago, that people who thought their city was beautiful were 28 percent more likely to trust the police. Though perhaps more a correlation than causation, she said, the finding nevertheless suggested that aesthetics in design do matter. For example, if the public library seems intimidating and it's also a polling place, some people might not enter to vote. A library, a park building, or a police station may be the core asset within a neighborhood, so it is well worth transforming it into something more relevant to the community it serves than it was before.

Parks have a particularly important role to play in the cohesiveness of a community, said Stewart. Parks are places for art, conversations, and cultural activities that are welcoming and reflective, he said, so we need to think about them "less as ornamentation, but as critical infrastructure components, not just from an ecological or environmental standpoint, but also for a social and cultural purpose."

Irizarry said Friends of the Parks, a nonprofit dedicated to preserving and improving the parks and open spaces in Chicago, looks at parks as democratic spaces from a design and landscape architecture point of view. But as neighborhoods gentrify, or as investment is put into a park, the group often hears from the community that while the space may be more beautiful, the people no longer feel it is for them. There are two extremes, she said. If violence or perceived security issues surround a park, people may be hesitant to engage that space. On the other hand, a park can be renovated and improved to the point that neighborhood folks wonder whether it's still actually for them. "It would be nice if the parks were places where people really develop trust, but sometimes, the way the process is happening, it's actually causing more distrust," Irizarry said. How do we get people to care enough about their parks not just to use them but to participate in planning and programming? One of the Friends of the Parks' roles has been to organize and support park advisory councils, which she said help people feel a sense of community ownership of their parks. The panel would later return to discussing such organized public engagement structures and processes in detail.

Stewart agreed that park officials have a duty in the design and programming of public spaces to create an environment that is safe and welcoming but also invites difficult socioeconomic conversations. The founding philosophy of Millennium Park, he said, was that it be free, open access, and representative of the democratic character of Chicago. Those attributes may be lost during the development or redevelopment of a park, leaving a community with an aesthetically beautiful and even useful public space that still fails to foster social and economic conversations that rise to the level of cultural community discourse.

Aguilar, an artist who works in urban public spaces and also mentors young students to do so, said freedom of expression may be curtailed when programming is tied to public funding or to private foundation money. De facto censorship and limits to artistic statement may be imposed in deference to the funding source, he said, which frustrates the youth, who want to express themselves freely. As a society, "we expect art to be always beautiful, always uplifting, always celebratory. What do we, as complex human beings, do with all our other emotions? Where is the art that represents us wholly, fully?" Teenagers, he noted, have a wide range of emotions and need spaces to explore all of them through art.

Another factor contributing to the tension between the individual artist and public expectations is a widespread misunderstanding of the artistic process and the incorrect but normative notion that artists work in the same linear way that designers do. Artists, Aguilar said, "do not know ten steps ahead exactly what the design is going to look like," and in fact the most highly respected artists "have no idea what's going on until it's finished." How, he asked, do we give students an authentic artistic experience, if we assign them what the end product is to look like? If they hope someday to create commissioned works in public spaces, perhaps that is an authentic experience.

WHOSE PARK IS IT?

Perhaps the majority of conflicts over a public space hinge on whether that asset is conceived primarily as hard infrastructure, aimed at fostering economic development, or as soft infrastructure, to benefit the quality of life and enjoyment of its community. Layered upon that (possibly false) dichotomy are questions of range and reach: How broadly and deeply will the economic benefits extend, and from how far will most users come for the soft attributes?

The critically acclaimed Millennium Park, opened in 2004 at a cost of $475 million, faces those questions on the grandest scale. Now the top tourist destination in the Midwest, with twenty million annual visitors, the park was actually conceived of as "all of Chicago's" park, said Stewart, executive director of the park's foundation. Loop dwellers use it as a neighborhood park. Starting long before the park opened, civic leaders wrestled with whether the twenty-five-acre park is primarily for the tourism economy or for the cultural identity in Chicago. The foundation sits at the juncture between the park and the private donors who helped get it built after the project exceeded its planned budget by a factor of three. Stewart said it's his job to manage the "red tape and expectations" that come with private funding. But the aim, he said, is always to create a park that best reflects the cultural identity of all of Chicago in its art, architecture, and cultural experiences.

To meet those goals, programming is crucial, Stewart said, and has been greatly improved since the park's opening. The Department of Cultural Affairs and Special Events has steered the programming so that "not only visitors to Chicago but also people of the neighborhoods can begin to see themselves better reflected within Millennium Park and see the park as part of their cultural sphere," said Stewart, perhaps not intentionally alluding to some of the iconic fixtures of the park, like the rounded mirrored surface of "the Bean" and the video images behind the Crown Fountain. The park was constructed, he said, "in a very traditional mind-set," as a "high-culture park, with high art and high architecture." But iconic status brings cultural barriers, and breaking down those perceived barriers has become the primary focus for programming.

Whether a park or public program is relevant and welcoming to its community depends on more than aesthetics. Access is a first consideration. Transportation is the number-one challenge for teens and preteens trying to get to a sport or arts program, Aguilar said, and the CTA is not a solution. Inviting parents helps, as does meeting at night or on weekends. Such measures risk burning out the staff, he admitted, but may be necessary.

An adjustment to both time and place solved access issues for a neighborhood library in Philadelphia that was working with Biagi. Her firm had analyzed the availability of services at different times of the day and days of the week at various civic assets. The library was delivering an effective job training program, but it was only offered nine to five, Monday through Friday, and many working people who wanted training could not attend. Down the street, however, a park was open evenings and weekends. Thinking about the park and library as being connected—and allowing some programming to cross the boundary—enabled the city to deliver job training to more people who wanted it. This type of cooperative approach may require expanding the core competencies of staffs.

Costs—often including transportation—are an obvious barrier to access and participation. Should a concert held in a public park be affordable for the people in that neighborhood? Millennium Park concerts are free, Irizarry noted, but parking is expensive, as is transit fare for large families. Stewart said park authorities had discussed charging a few dollars for events so that money could be shifted to providing transportation, just as many public spaces across the country have begun looking at ways to generate revenue due to current budget constraints and a whole gamut of financial needs. But fees would violate the core mission of Millennium Park, Stewart said, which is to provide cultural experiences for free. Funding free programming, and keeping it free of overcommercialization, he said, is the work of the foundation, at the interface between private donors and the city.

FOLLOW THE MONEY

Some Chicago Park District venues and programming do generate revenue, and how that revenue is prioritized and dispersed among the city's parks can be controversial. Revenue just from the rental of Soldier Field (including to the Chicago Bears), the Northerly Island concert pavilion, and other park district facilities was projected to be $35.8 million for fiscal year 2017. Some major events are held in outlying parks, but Irizarry said the neighborhoods are not always seeing the financial returns to their own parks. According to Biagi, New York City is grappling with issues of park equity because its signature parks, Central Park and Battery Park, have drawn most of the philanthropic donations. Those funds need to be leveraged for the other parks, where major donors have little incentive to contribute.

Balancing investment between large and small parks is essential. The economic impact study of parks in Chicago, the most extensive done in any city,

Biagi said, looked at all of the parks and each one's influence on property values within a two-block radius. It found that Chicago parks, on average, added 1.5 percent to nearby property values—a large effect, she said. But the small parks, even if run-down and in need of repair, added 3.5 percent, helping to stabilize their neighborhoods.

Returning to Stewart's earlier point that parks play a role in the cohesiveness of a community, Salomon asked if community art and architecture can address violence, a major issue in Chicago. Neighborhood parks are sometimes the site of gang activity and violence, but parks and other public spaces can be designed and programmed so as to have a calming effect. Biagi's firm worked on a project in the North Lawndale neighborhood that brought police together with groups like Black Lives Matter to find ways to build trust and whether design might have a role. One small idea emerged—installing a basketball hoop on a police station parking lot, which provided access to kids who were cut off from their parks by gang lines. Two years later, the police tweeted out a video of officers playing ball with youngsters under the hashtags #BuildingBridges and #BuildingPeace.

Irizarry said that because La Villita Park—the park that Ross Barney mentioned, built on a brownfield near the river—is higher than street level, drive-by shootings are less of a concern. Residents of Little Village have organized around that space and engaged youth through sports and other activities. The local kids now feel ownership, she said, and the community organizers have moved on to the next park to repeat the process.

Making neighborhood families feel ownership of their parks—by a variety of means—and keeping them engaged from planning through programming and maintenance were discussed at length by the panel. Irizarry said that community residents may initially be excited by a project that portends economic opportunity for the neighborhood but grow disillusioned if priorities shift toward revenue or tourism benefits downtown. People may dig in and fight for what they think is best for their neighborhood, she said, or withdraw if they feel powerless.

One example of reaction to community promises was playing out that very day regarding the Obama Presidential Center, sited partly on public land in Jackson Park. People camped out in front of where the Obama Foundation was meeting to demand a community-benefits agreement, to guarantee that benefits derive to the people who already live there. Another recent example, Irizarry said, was the 606 or Bloomingdale Trail, connecting Northwest Side neighborhoods to the Chicago River and several city boulevards. Comprising six neighborhood parks, a plaza, an observatory, and art installations, the elevated 2.7-mile trail transformed an obsolete rail embankment into a green corridor for active cycling, walking, and jogging. But officials may have failed in reaching out to existing community residents prior to its opening in 2015. Irizarry, who said she lived along the trail for forty-five years, went to neighborhood meetings during the planning for the 606 and didn't see any other Latinos. "A lot of folks just opted out early on," she said. Puerto Ricans in Humboldt Park had already watched gentrification march westward and knew that "community planning is not for us, so why should we bother?" She herself moved away, and many low-income renters were economically displaced by the new amenity.

Biagi said that community organizing, especially with its roots in Chicago, should occur not only in reaction to a specific project but rather to prepare a community for any opportunity or crisis that arises. Ideally, she said, funders would allow communities "to define what capacities they need to build, and how they're going to organize, and not ask them to line up with what we like to fund."

Effective voices of community interests, Irizarry said, are the individual Park Advisory Councils (PACs), representing about a third of Chicago's 600 parks. Sometimes the only community organization in an area, sometimes an outgrowth of an existing advocacy group, PACs are for anyone who cares about their park, she said, such as parents who think the local playground needs to be rehabbed. PACs try to keep the focus on neighborhood needs rather than revenue generation, Irizarry said, but park district officials often receive those PACs that agree with them differently from those that do not. She wished officials would see the PACs as partners, not as threats.

Not just money but also attention and programming should flow from downtown to outlying neighborhoods, several panelists said. "There are kids in the city who have never been to the lake and only see downtown from a distance," Biagi said. "Sometimes we have to bring services out to them." Stewart said he has challenged the Millennium Park curatorial committee to forgo internationally recognized artists and showcase Chicago artists instead and to use interpretive signage and other devices to direct visitors into the neighborhoods to see local artworks in their natural venue. "This is a major pivot for the Millennium Park philosophy," he said.

Aguilar noted that many private institutions that are "downtown centric" struggle to engage in short-term initiatives in different communities and may partner with neighborhood organizations. But he drew hearty audience applause when he admonished private organizations and city officials alike:

"Don't 'perform' community engagement by staging public sessions to rein-force the agenda you already have. Sit down, shut up, and actually listen."

CONNECTING PEOPLE AND PLACES: DESIGNING TRANSPORTATION SYSTEMS FOR SMART CITIES

For the rest of the day, the Urban Forum turned its attention to transpor-tation infrastructure, first with a panel discussion and then with a closing keynote by Illinois transportation secretary Randy Blankenhorn. The panel was moderated by WBEZ reporter and producer Miles Bryan and featured Leanne Redden, executive director of the Regional Transportation Authority; MarySue Barrett, president of the Metropolitan Planning Council; Clayton Harris III, executive director of the Illinois International Port District (IDOT, often referred to as the Port of Chicago); and Rob Burke, executive director of the Active Transportation Alliance.

Bryan began the conversation on a sore point, a topic of no controversy among the discussants: money, or rather the severe lack of it, for the Chi-cago region's transportation needs. Noting the unforeseen absence of any federal infrastructure bill, Bryan asked the panelists, perhaps cruelly, to imagine nonetheless how they would have spent the large sums that were not forthcoming. How should transportation funding mechanisms be re-structured?

Perhaps knowing the head of IDOT was to follow them, the panelists largely ignored the fanciful first part of Bryan's question and focused in-stead on the second: idealizing funding mechanisms. Redden, who heads the parent transit company that coordinates budgets and planning for the CTA, the Metra regional commuter rail system, and the Pace suburban bus system, said the federal government needs to come up with real money. She said that in the Chicago region, state and local transportation officials had already leveraged all they could out of limited federal money. "Private-equity money, gimmicks, and tax credits" will not meet the long-term needs of the region, which has the second-largest transit system in the United States and an economy historically based on transportation, she said. Revenues gener-ated by transit fares cannot be diverted into capital projects because they are needed entirely for operations. State and local officials must make the case to their federal counterparts that spending on transportation offers a return on investment, and not just in terms of jobs. As noted in the Urban Forum essay by Beverly Bunch, increased supply-chain costs, delays in personal travel and commuting, and other factors resulting from infrastructure deficiencies are estimated to cost the average American family a loss of $3,400 in disposable income annually between 2016 and 2025.

Barrett, whose organization works with government and the private sector on regional planning, said pleading the federal case was necessary but probably not sufficient. "It's never a good strategy to wait for Washington," she said. "Now more than ever, we're in an era of self-help." As an example of local partnership, she cited the modernization of the CTA's Red and Purple train lines, which needs $43 billion for the largest capital-upgrade project in CTA history. At the end of the Obama administration, $1.1 billion was available for the first phase of the Red and Purple Modernization (RPM) program, but the required local matching funds were not forthcoming. In 2016 the state legislature approved a transit tax-increment financing district around the project zone to capture future revenue growth from property values. The transit TIF, which Barrett said was specially structured so as not to divert tax revenues from Chicago's public schools, established a long-term local funding mechanism and allowed the CTA to capture federal funds to begin the first phase of RPM.

Harris said the Port District, which he called the greatest multimodal facility in North America, needs capital and would be willing to take it from anybody. He expressed dismay that the governor recently vetoed a bill that would have erased half of the port's $30 million in debt—the portion the state wrote off thirty-six years ago when planned improvements were not made. Taking the debt off the books would finally help the port borrow funds again. The port, he said, generates at least $27 million annually in state revenue and $157 million in federal revenue.

Burke, whose advocacy group a few years ago expanded its focus from bicycling and walking to also include transit, held out little hope for federal transit funding, especially under a Trump administration. "Just as federal and state agriculture policy is hard-wired to grow corn, federal and state transportation policy is hard-wired to grow highways," he said, which does not relieve congestion but exacerbates it. He said he hoped that the Chicago Metropolitan Agency for Planning (CMAP), representing seven northeastern Illinois counties, would shift its long-term goals more toward new transportation modes, a change that will require local funding. Denver and even Los Angeles have imposed taxes to fund transit systems, he said, and the Chicago region likewise needs to find new local revenues to expand and maintain transit for the sake of transportation equity and the environment.

HUNKER DOWN OR FORGE AHEAD?

Bryan asked the panel how, during a time of such tight public funding, transportation officials should balance everyday maintenance and operations with exciting new projects. Burke observed that bike projects are inexpensive; the more than one hundred miles of advanced bike lanes and other amenities installed in Chicago over the past eight years cost less than $30 million—a "rounding error" compared to a highway or transit project. Redden said the Regional Transportation Authority decided years ago to forgo new expansion and focus on stewardship of existing infrastructure, spending only $800,000 each year instead of the $2–$3 billion a prudent maintenance schedule would require. Harris said that the port, hidden as it is from the public, is not concerned with upgrading front-facing amenities, as the RTA is, but must focus on the underlying integrity of its assets to ensure coordination among all modes.

In his forthcoming keynote, Blankenhorn, who before leaving to head IDOT was executive director of CMAP, would likewise endorse the conservative, maintenance-focused approach for transit, building "only on the margins; we have the systems we're going to have." But countering her copanelists, Barrett expressed the contrary view. "We can't sell people on maintenance," she said. "We need to tie maintenance together with excitement about what's next." Already suffering low ridership, transit faces new threats from shared services like Lyft and Uber. Still, Barrett said, two-thirds of people get into the Loop by transit. "Google said they would not have located their new facility in the West Loop but for the new Morgan Street station," she said, and the other new station designed by Ross Barney, at Cermak on the South Side, also supports new job centers and mixed-use centers. "So we have to tell people, 'Here are the next five Metra stations to be upgraded, and CTA stations, and the next bus rapid-transit route, and a Lake Shore Drive multimodal dedicated lane.'" Such forward-looking projects, she said, inspired citizens and lawmakers in Denver, Los Angeles, and other cities to dedicate local funding for public transportation growth.

ALL ABOARD

Bryan asked the transportation panel to turn to a topic explored by the earlier panel on parks: How do you make sure you have broad public input and engagement and consider users in all strata of society? Redden said the RTA must weigh broad social equity and access issues all the time and therefore does not operate as efficiently as it otherwise could. "It's a trade-off," she said. "People say we should run it like a business, but it's not meant to run like a business. The [public] transit system we have came from the private sector when they couldn't afford to run it anymore."

Burke said local voices are the most powerful and knowledgeable. The city's bike-share vendor faced criticism for locating its bike docks in predominantly upscale and commercial areas. But Burke said lower-income communities want a focus on transit, not bikes, as few good jobs are nearby and residents say they can't afford to get to others. To that end, his organization has been working with a South Side community coalition to persuade Metra and RTA to operate the Metra Electric line more like the CTA, with more stops and more frequent service. As jobs continue to move outward in the suburbs, he said, we will continue to struggle to connect lower-income people to them.

A member of the audience asked the panel to elaborate further on suburban transit. Burke said the suburbs, built for cars only, need to make their streets more bike friendly. Expanding rail is not feasible in the short term. Pace, the suburban bus service, has made progress with express buses, but needs to move buses faster and add more stops. Barrett added that the area's tollways should accommodate buses in the right-of-way, just as a few of the freeways already do, on their shoulders. "There is clear demand for suburban transit," she said. "But we don't provide enough of it to know what the actual demand for it is."

The Urban Forum's finale was a solo by Blankenhorn, who echoed themes heard in the transportation panel but added some new notes as well. Burke had earlier cited figures that only about 13 percent of people in the region get where they're going by transit and only about 28 percent even within the city. Ninety percent of suburban trips are by car. As head of IDOT, Blankenhorn oversees an agency of forty-eight hundred employees, a $3 billion operating budget, and $3.4 billion in capital projects—including roadwork. He also brought into consideration some of the most disruptive new technologies and networked services that will come in the years ahead and will arrive by car.

He began as the panelists did, by considering funding mechanisms. Unlike the previous discussants, he thinks the Trump administration is interested in providing more federal dollars and will find new ways to structure federal support. Washington, he predicted, will continue to provide only limited, targeted funding and perhaps not the first dollars into a project but the last, to close the gaps—an approach that would restructure the relationship between the federal and state and local governments.

Thirty percent of all transportation funding is federal, and Blankenhorn favors an increase in the motor-fuel tax at the federal level—an unlikely development, the Illinois congressional delegation has told him. As noted in the Bunch chapter, Congress has not raised the motor-fuel tax rate since 1993, and shortfalls in the Highway Trust Fund have deepened as gasoline consumption has dropped due to vehicles' improved fuel efficiency and people driving less.

Instead, the federal government is looking for new ways to leverage private funding for infrastructure. Blankenhorn said public-private partnerships make sense in some roles but not in most. As Bunch wrote, P3s are feasible for projects that generate a revenue stream, such as toll roads and airports, but are less likely to work for the non-revenue-generating and smaller infrastructure projects that make up the bulk of state and local capital spending.

Despite the limitations of P3s, IDOT nonetheless constantly looks for ways to use them, Blankenhorn said. The Chicago Region Environmental and Transportation Efficiency (CREATE) program, an ongoing seventy-project $4.4 billion plan to improve freight, commuter, and intercity passenger rail movement and reduce driving delays, was the first big P3 in the United States and a way for city, state, and federal transportation authorities to leverage private money from the railroads. A third of the funds have been committed, and nearly three-fourths of the projects are completed or under way.

Another federal P3 is the Infrastructure for Rebuilding America competitive-grant program, for which Blankenhorn said Chicago has a strong proposal. Along the Seventy-Fifth Street corridor, conflicts between freight rail, Amtrak, Metra, and the highway system create perhaps the biggest rail pinch point in the country, he said. The proposal to remediate the corridor seeks less than a third of the money from the federal government, with the rest coming from state and local sources and the railroads.

Another proposed project, one not yet approved by the state legislature, would add a fee-based managed lane to the Stevenson Expressway (Interstate 55) alongside the existing toll-free lanes, giving drivers the option to pay to get to or from downtown in less time. Congestion pricing is yet another approach, Blankenhorn said. Differential pricing structures are already utilized on highways all over the world, he said; Illinois is behind the times.

What is politically impossible in Washington might work in Springfield; state revenues for transportation could be generated with an additional motor-fuel tax, said Blankenhorn, a believer in "the user pays." Illinois needs long-term sustainable funding for its day-to-day needs, he said. Borrowing money for big new projects that will last fifty years makes sense, but thirty years of debt for one that will last eight years does not. "That's what we're doing now, and we need to get away from it," he said.

Driving Blankenhorn's search for a source of continuous local funding is a pressing need to rebuild the Eisenhower Expressway, Interstate 290, one of the most congested highways in the United States. When it was built fifty years ago, the Ike split the neighborhoods it passed through. Rebuilding the expressway is an opportunity to reconnect communities, with overpasses that boast plazas and parks and retail that will make them not just bridges but attractions in their own right. "This is our chance to build a truly twenty-first-century expressway, and we can't lose the opportunity," Blankenhorn said. Transportation professionals have gone from ignoring the soft side of their infrastructure to realizing the need to accommodate bikes and pedestrians and transit and to incorporate community development from beginning to end, he said.

A similar encompassing view needs to be taken in a redo of Lake Shore Drive, another major project in the long-range plans. Blankenhorn said Chicago's lakefront corridor needs to accommodate bikes and pedestrians and connect with the parkland, and it will need to move people in a different way. Initially, IDOT's project planners, along with the city and other partners, narrowed the options too far, on the basis of cost, he said. But since there isn't funding to do this today anyway, he said, "we need to think bigger, about an ultimate solution that makes our jewel of a lakefront work for everyone." The transportation systems of the past are not the systems of the future, he said, and even the goals are not the same.

Transportation agencies need to change, according to Blankenhorn. They need to be more creative, including about funding. They need to encourage broader participation and talk to people about what transportation means to them, to their community, and to their quality of life.

Technology will change transportation in ways we've barely begun to think about, Blankenhorn believes, and driverless vehicles are coming. Earlier, in response to an audience question to the panel, Burke cited a study by TransitCenter, a New York foundation dedicated to urban mobility, that said no such technology could replace public transportation, at least in dense urban centers. "You can't move the number of people we move with public transit in personal automobiles, autonomous or not," Burke explained. "But they do eat into ridership."

Blankenhorn convened a task force of state agencies, including IDOT, the secretary of state, and the Department of Insurance, to resolve a host of issues that will arrive with driverless cars, such as who is at fault in an accident, the human or the vehicle? He believes IDOT needs to provide an opportunity for testing, which may best be done first on commercial vehicles, like trucks. "Illinois moves a lot of freight, and we want to work with the companies that want to try this," he said. "We want the research to happen here and in our academic institutions." But make no mistake: autonomous-vehicle technology is coming. "It's not *The Jetsons*," he said.

Revolutionary transportation technology looms large on the horizon. But what is that other apparition off in the distance? Is it a federal infrastructure bill? Or just a mirage? Months after the Urban Forum, in early 2018 the White House announced a plan to raise $1.5 trillion over ten years for infrastructure, with $200 billion coming from federal funds. A poll by the Hornstein Center around that time found that three-fourths of Americans believed improvements were needed and worth funding. But where would Congress find the money, after 2017's massive tax cut? A separate poll around that time found an increase to the gas tax to be not popular at all. Democrats lofted their own trillion-dollar infrastructure plan in March and proposed to pay for the federal contribution by restoring much of the revenues lost in the Republican tax overhaul. Amid mounting political turmoil on several unrelated fronts, as this book went to press, the fate of the nation's public infrastructure was no clearer than it was on a sunny Thursday last September when the 2017 Urban Forum took place.

[blank page 144]

Contributors

PHILIP ASHTON is associate professor of urban planning and policy at the University of Illinois at Chicago. Ashton's research and practice focus on the restructuring of U.S. retail finance, with a consistent interest in how minority borrowers and neighborhoods have fared in the "new financial marketplace." This has translated into research projects on subprime mortgage lending and the racialization of credit risk, the foreclosure crisis and its governance, and the role of investment banks and infrastructure funds in producing the growing market for urban infrastructure assets. He is currently working on a book project on fraud and discrimination litigation against large subprime mortgage lenders.

BEVERLY BUNCH is a professor in the Public Administration Program at the University of Illinois at Springfield with a joint appointment in the Center for State Policy and Leadership. Her areas of expertise are state budgeting and the financing of capital infrastructure. She has published in journals such as *Public Budgeting and Finance, Public Administration Review,* and the *Municipal Finance Journal.* She has a Ph.D. in public policy from Carnegie Mellon University and a master's in public administration from the Maxwell School at Syracuse University.

BILL BURTON, a freelance writer, is former director of public affairs at the University of Illinois at Chicago and was a science writer at the University of Chicago and Northwestern University. A graduate of McGill University in Montreal, he received his Ph.D. in biochemistry from the University of

Illinois at Urbana-Champaign and served a media fellowship through the American Association for the Advancement of Science.

CHARLES HOCH is professor emeritus of urban planning and policy at the University of Illinois at Chicago. Hoch has taught urban planning at the University of Illinois at Chicago since 1981. He studies how professional planners and others make spatial plans and the kind of work plans do. He has taught courses on the history, theory, organization, and practice of planning using pragmatist ideas.

Hoch has written several books on the conduct of planning, most recently with Frank So and Linda Dalton, editing *The Practice of Local Government Planning* (2000), as well as authoring *What Planners Do: Power, Politics and Persuasion* (1994). He has also published research on housing and community development, including *Under One Roof,* edited with George Hemmens and Jana Carp (1996), and authoring with Robert Slayton *New Homeless and Old: Community and the Skid Row Hotel* (1989). Hoch has published articles on planning theory, practice, and housing in the *Journal of the American Planning Association,* the *Journal of Planning Education and Research,* the *Journal of Architectural and Planning Research, Planning Theory, Planning Theory and Practice, Plan Canada, Town Planning Review,* and other social science journals.

Prior to joining UIC's College of Urban Planning and Public Affairs, Hoch taught at Iowa State University. He received his doctorate in urban planning from the University of California, Los Angeles.

SEAN LALLY is an associate professor of architecture at the University of Illinois at Chicago. Lally is the author of the book *The Air from Other Planets: A Brief History of Architecture to Come* (2014). He is the host of the podcast *Night White Skies.* Lally is the founder of Weathers, a Chicago-based design office of architects, landscape architects, engineers, and researchers. He is the recipient of the Prince Charitable Trust's Rome Prize from the American Academy in Rome in landscape architecture and the winner of the Architectural League Prize for Young Architects and Designers Award. Lally has a master's of architecture from the University of California, Los Angeles, and a bachelor of science in landscape architecture from the University of Massachusetts at Amherst.

SANJEEV VIDYARTHI is an associate professor of urban planning and policy at the University of Illinois at Chicago. Trained as an architect, urban designer, and spatial planner, Vidyarthi's research interests span the fields of planning theory and history, globalization, and development studies. Exploring planning and designing efforts across spatial scales in a variety of urban settings, such as neighborhoods, new towns, historic cities, and urban regions, his scholarly work focuses on the meanings and purposes of planning for places. Sanjeev has lived, worked, and studied in the Middle East, western Europe, and the United States apart from India, a case he studies using a comparative lens and an insider-outsider perspective.

[blank page 148]

THE URBAN AGENDA

Metropolitan Resilience in a Time of Economic Turmoil
  Edited by Michael A. Pagano

Technology and the Resilience of Metropolitan Regions
  Edited by Michael A. Pagano

The Return of the Neighborhood as an Urban Strategy
  Edited by Michael A. Pagano

Remaking the Urban Social Contract: Health, Energy, and the Environment
  Edited by Michael A. Pagano

Jobs and the Labor Force of Tomorrow: Migration, Training, Education
  Edited by Michael A. Pagano

The Public Infrastructure of Work and Play
  Edited by Michael A. Pagano

The University of Illinois Press
is a founding member of the
Association of American University Presses.

———————————————————————

Composed in 10.5/13 Minion Pro
with Franklin Gothic display
by Lisa Connery
at the University of Illinois Press
Cover design by Dustin J. Hubbart
Manufactured by Sheridan Books, Inc.

University of Illinois Press
1325 South Oak Street
Champaign, IL 61820-6903
www.press.uillinois.edu